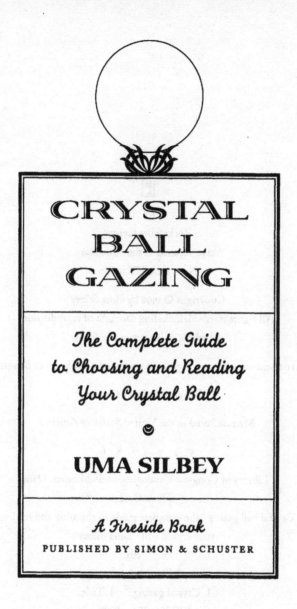

CRYSTAL BALL GAZING

The Complete Guide to Choosing and Reading Your Crystal Ball

UMA SILBEY

A Fireside Book

PUBLISHED BY SIMON & SCHUSTER

FIRESIDE
Rockefeller Center
1230 Avenue of the Americas
New York, NY 10020

Copyright © 1998 by Uma Silbey
All rights reserved, including the right of reproduction
in whole or in part in any form.

FIRESIDE and colophon are registered trademarks of Simon & Schuster Inc.

Designed by Jenny Dossin

Manufactured in the United States of America

5   7   9   10   8   6

Library of Congress Cataloging-in-Publication Data
Silbey, Uma.
Crystal ball gazing : the complete guide to choosing and reading
your crystal ball / Uma Silbey.
p.   cm.
A Fireside book.
1. Crystal gazing.   I. Title.
BF1335.S54   1998
133.'22—dc21   98-14381
                                    CIP

ISBN-13: 978-0-684-83644-7
ISBN-10:   0-684-83644-0

To my husband, Steve, for his love, his belief in me and his heart-felt support that he has given me throughout our life together. Thank you with all my heart.

☙

To my children, Ram Paul and Luke. Hopefully, I've exposed you to things that will enrich your entire lives. Thank you for your unconditional love . . . and I love you so much.

☙

To all of my beloved teachers who have provided me with insight and spiritual direction. Most specifically I wish to thank Neem Karoli Baba Ji, Kalu Rimpoche, Grandfather Bearheart, Yogi Bhajan, and Daniel. May you be blessed.

☙

To all of the members, past and present, of UMA Jewelry, Music and Books who have helped me in the manifestation of my vision throughout the years, and thus have helped so many others in countless ways.

"We begin life with the world presenting itself to us as it is. Someone—our parents, teachers, analysts—hypnotizes us to 'see' the world and construe it in the 'right' way. These others label the world, attach names and give voices to the beings and events in it, so that thereafter, we cannot read the world in any other language or hear it saying other things to us. The task is to break the hypnotic spell, so that we become undeaf, unblind, and multilingual, thereby letting the world speak to us in new voices and write all its possible meaning in the new book of our existence."

SIDNEY JOURARD *from* Sunbeams

CONTENTS

9

CHAPTER THREE
Choosing, Storing, and Charging Your Crystal Ball

CHAPTER SIX
Doorways to Other Worlds

INTRODUCTION

A New Generation of Seers

I grew up in what I would describe as a very "sensible" family, though I must say we do have more than our share of artists and musicians. I suppose, like most of you, I had what you would call a fairly conventional childhood. I certainly didn't grow up thinking that I would one day be an ardent crystal ball gazer! My only early contact with crystal ball reading was through pictures I'd seen of Gypsies wearing exotic garb and looking otherworldly. It was not until my late twenties that I was introduced to the use of crystal balls in any serious way, and what I discovered then was quite a surprise.

I was studying the Cabbalah with a rather extraordinary teacher. This was in the seventies, before people were getting interested in crystals. My teacher invited me to come to a meditation group of maybe six or eight people, who were experimenting with the different effects of these stones. We were putting them in different formations, sending sound through them, learning about their subtle energy fields and how they might be useful for meditation, healing, and stimulating intuition or creativity.

One day, our teacher pulled out a glass ball, very clear and transparent. Nobody else in the room seemed very interested, but I could not take my eyes from it. To me, it was beautiful. As I gazed into it I noticed a tiny bubble at the center. I remember the room was relatively dark at the time, but there was a ray of light going through the ball and it became like a golden sun sitting on the table.

As I looked inside the ball, the bubble at the center seemed to be transformed in my mind's eye. I saw the bubble as a beautiful planet floating in clear space, so I got this otherworldly feeling from it. After quite a long time, our teacher turned his attention to me.

"You seem very interested in that," he said. "Let's take a closer look."

He moved the glass ball to the center of the table and I sat down opposite him. He just asked me to pay attention to what I was seeing in the ball. I told him, "I feel like I'm in outer space, like an astronaut. When I focus on the bubble it just seems to draw me inside, and I feel like I've traveled far beyond the earth."

He then moved the light a little closer to the ball and I had the sensation of just traveling off into this other realm, feeling very open and free. I was deeply, deeply moved by the experience, in a way that was difficult to describe.

That night as the group was breaking up and getting ready to go home, my teacher came over and pressed the glass ball into my hand. "Here," he said. "I think this should be yours."

I was incredulous. I could not believe that he was giving me this wonderful present. I was so dazzled by his unexpected gift that I'm not sure I even properly thanked him.

I took the ball home with me and set it up with a little stand on a table in my bedroom. I'd move it to different places in the house, usually in those places where I particularly liked to hang out. And occasionally I'd find myself gazing into the ball.

At the same period of time I had been learning about crystal gazing, that is, with natural crystals. We would set up a large crystal in a darkened room and beam a strong light on it. The people I was with were practicing time travel and out-of-body experiences. I thought it all very intriguing but I was also quite skeptical.

In spite of my doubts, I was hooked. I would gaze into the crystal with the rest of our group and from time to time I'd get strong impressions, but, unlike most of the others, I didn't really see specific images. I became frustrated.

When I went home after these sessions with the crystal, I would gaze into the glass ball. I felt a bit inadequate because I was apparently not seeing what others in my meditation group were seeing, but the impressions I was getting were extremely interesting. I would just gaze into the ball and feel very free, almost as if I were flying or floating weightlessly in space.

I was amazed by the level of concentration I could get as I gazed into the ball. I found I could sit for longer and longer periods of time, just letting my mind float. I'd always used my mind a lot, creating, writing, and speaking. With the ball, however, I could concentrate completely yet be totally free of having to do something. I had begun to have experiences that I had never had during even the deepest meditations. Moreover, using the ball I could get into a deep meditative state much faster than I'd ever been able to do with any other meditation technique. I would look into the ball and move right into a wonderful, centered, free, and open healing space.

Gradually I started using the ball to get myself focused for whatever decisions or tasks I was involved with at the time. This kind of focus was valuable whether I was paying my bills, writing a book, or simply getting grounded. Not long after that I began to use it to help me get new perspectives on issues in my life. I began asking questions and then using the ball to empty my mind and open up to new possibilities. The questions I tended to ask mostly had to do with everyday living—relationships, job, where I wanted to live. I would ask to see different viewpoints. And I found that by working with the glass ball I would free my own mind enough to experience these other viewpoints.

Today I usually do readings just for myself. I've found that crystal balls are wonderful for training the mind, teaching us to shift from a rational, linear way of thinking, to use both sides of our brains more. I've found through my work with the crystal ball that I've become much more intuitive. Also, I'm a person who always has lots of projects going on. I really need to focus quickly and completely on each thing I'm doing, so that it can be done well, in a clear, relaxed, and creatively satisfying way. Crystal ball gazing has helped me to concentrate like this. I particularly like to use the crystal ball when I'm designing jewelry or writing. It frees my mind so that I'm open to totally new possibilities. I'm always surprised by what I discover. As often as not, it's like that old expression of ideas coming from left field. Sometimes they're useful, sometimes they're not. But they always jar me out of my set way of thinking and provide me with a fresh perspective.

In any event, when we learn how to make use of the crystal ball in the ways I've tried to describe for you in this book, life suddenly becomes more fascinating and richer because we can open ourselves up to creative avenues in virtually every area of life—in personal development, relationships, career, art, spiritual development—the list goes on and on. But even more than that, divination with a crystal ball can offer a way to open a window, if only a very small one, onto possibilities beyond the often hard realities of our everyday lives.

As a tool for making our lives fuller, freer, and even easier, your crystal ball can become one of the most valuable guides you possess, like a warm and trusted friend who is there for you in all of life's endless challenges.

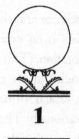

1

Crystals and Energy

VIBRATION AND SUBTLE ENERGY

When I was learning to work with crystals, crystal balls, and stones, I practiced many, many methods. Most were supported by centuries of tradition. Some, on the surface, seemed to contradict each other. So my main work in learning, looking back, was how to integrate these apparent contradictions by searching for the essence that ties them all together.

What forms the essence or basis of crystal, gemstone, and crystal ball work, whether it be the work of the ancient shaman, the mystic, the Gypsy, or the everyday person, is *energy*. Just as science uses the crystal for its piezoelectric qualities, mystics and others use it for its amplifying and other qualities. Either way, whether scientific or traditional, all are using the quartz crystal for making changes on an energetic level.

Modern physicists have affirmed that tangible form consists, in essence, not of matter but of energy—and that the nature of physical material is intrinsically dynamic, in process. The same is true with thoughts and feelings which are interwoven and interdependent. Though we can't see them, both can be scientifically understood and measured in the form of ever-moving, vibrating waves of energy. Electromagnetism, electricity, sound, light, and other forms of energy also exist as measurable, yet invisible, vibrating waves. According to both science and the ancient teachings, ultimately everything that exists is an external manifestation of an energy form, expressed as vibration. (This mustn't be misunderstood to mean that there is no soul. On the contrary, soul or "God" is beyond and within all form.) Each form differs in the way it manifests because it differs vibrationally. The slower the rate of vibration, the denser the form; the quicker the rate, the lighter the form.

Classic yoga and other such forms of instruction teach that entire bodies and worlds exist with such a fine or quick rate of vibration that they can't be experienced by our more dense physical senses, but only by other ways of perceiving that we gain when we speed up or raise our vibrational rate. They teach that surrounding the physical body lie other subtle energy bodies that interrelate and influence each other and are invisible to our physical senses.

The first one is our electromagnetic body (the aura), which extends usually on a few inches from our physical body. The next is the more finely vibrating emotional (astral) body, followed by the even more highly vibrating mental, causal, and other bodies. According to these teachings, the mental/emotional and higher spiritual levels of man's consciousness help regulate each other through a subtle nervous system that we have within our bodies. This subtle-energy nervous system also receives, channels, and transmutes the basic universal life force that we need to live. The life force flows up and down our bodies through an etheric, central cord of energy that lies roughly along our spinal column to pierce through a series of whirling, disclike structures called "chakras." The seven major chakra areas correspond to the rectum (first chakra), sex organs (second chakra), navel point (third chakra), heart center (fourth chakra), the thyroid at the throat (fifth chakra), the pituitary at the forehead center ("third eye" or sixth center), and the top-center of the head or the anterior fontanel or pineal (seventh center). These chakras, connected to our physical, electromagnetic, astral, and other etheric bodies, when stimulated or "opened" transform frequencies of energy that, when transformed, bring better health and result in different behaviors and levels of consciousness. Working with crystals and crystal balls can stimulate these chakra areas, bringing a higher awareness and a sense of inner balance that not only helps you to "see" more in your crystal ball, but will help in other areas of your life. In the following chapters you will read about this process in much more detail.

☺

THE POWER OF CRYSTALS

Both the scientist and the mystic, then, teach that vibrationally, every form of manifestation is interrelated. Because of this essential interrelatedness, there is a cause-and-effect relationship where a vibrational change in one location creates a corresponding vibrational change in related locations. As a result of their structure, formation, and other qualities, quartz crystals can be precisely manipulated to change the vibration of almost anything with which they come in contact. In the electronics and computer industry, electrical impulses activate and direct the crystal. In crystal and crystal ball work, we use the vibration of our own thought waves, using focused intention to interact vibrationally with the crystal. Thus, quartz crystals and crystal balls can modify thoughts, emotions, our bodies, and other physical forms through various methods that vary between cultures and ages.

Science may claim that this is impossible, saying that it is scientifically unproven that you can feel vibration or influence vibratory changes with your mind, crystals, or in any other way. However, "scientific proof" only means that something has been shown to be true using scientific methods. People have been getting excellent results, scientifically proven or not for centuries, by being able to manipulate energy using crystals and crystal balls.

When you are crystal ball gazing, energy is an actual experience that you can physically feel in your hands and body and/or sense intuitively. The feeling is like a vibrating presence or sensation that constantly changes its frequency and temperature depending on what physical body, thought, or emotion it represents. Through the modification or transmutation of this energy using crystal balls combined with concentration and the knowledge of subtle energy, negative emotions can be transformed to positive. States of disharmony can be changed to harmony. Our bodies can be energized or healed. In place of stress we can generate calm. Thoughts can be amplified, increasing the power of affirmation, concentration, meditation, intention, and visualization. The uses and benefits of quartz crystals can extend as far as the limits of our vision.

BACKGROUND

Throughout history crystal ball gazing has sometimes flourished and sometimes been driven underground. Whether they called it a "spirit voice" or felt it as "vibration," gazers have been aware of some other force or energy that they were working with that allowed for the expanded vision that they received through crystal gazing and working with stones. Possibly this is one reason that people have long sensed something special about stones beyond their beauty. People have always been fascinated with stones, especially with those that are bright and glittery, like diamonds, sapphires, amethysts, emeralds, tourmalines, and aquamarines. From ancient times stones were experienced to have special energies and healing powers. Colors, shapes, and textures, as well as clarity, were also important. Crystals, however, throughout history have been the stones that people found most fascinating. From myths like Merlin's crystal cave to Superman's kryptonite to the crystal-mining dwarfs in "Snow White," stones generally, crystals and crystal balls specifically, appear over and over again as legend, tradition, and healing and spiritual practice. We see them in ancient amulets, power rings, chest plates, and bracelets. From the Hopis, the Hindus, Malaysians, Asians, Australian Aborigines, and others, we see crystals as hand-held power objects used for creators of intention, power boosters, and agents of change. Clear rock crystal was the most valued both because it was highly "energetic" and had clarity that allowed you to see most perfectly inside.

☺

PREHISTORIC AND SHAMANIC USE OF CRYSTAL AND CRYSTAL BALLS

Though some reports say that the use of stones, crystal, and crystal ball gazing as a method of divination developed sometime around 1000 B.C., it has actually been used in even earlier ages. Since their first memories, the Australian Aborigines have regarded a crystal as having magical properties that can be used to project the mind beyond the confines of space and time. In New South Wales the natives have carefully passed from generation to generation the information about the use of precious and semi-precious stones and especially quartz crystals in their rituals of healing and divination. To the Mayans the crystal was sacred to their god Tezcatlipoca and was used for both divining and healing. In Mexico there was a temple dedicated to this god that had walls lined with reflective crystalline stones. They also have used crystals, pyrites, and obsidian for gazing since their early times. The ancient Incas used both crystals and mirrors for gazing, often using them to judge the guilt and innocence of criminals. Many tribes in Africa used to gaze into water, mirrors, and crystals, some hand polished into rough sphere shapes.

Crystals and crystal balls have been used for healing, diagnosing the source of illnesses and other problems, foretelling the future and soul travel in North, Central, and South American shamanism. Within ancient native communities, the use of gem-stones, crystals, or crystal balls for scrying or divination was common long before the Europeans came to the continent. These native peoples have long gazed into polished crystals and consulted them for problem solving, healing, and divining the future. Many of these tribes still use these methods and there are still sacred teachers using this art.

❂

MIDDLE AND FAR EAST, CHINA AND GREECE

In ancient Rome, Greece, India, Egypt, Chaldea, Persia, and Palestine the priests made predictions by divination and were constantly consulted. Prophecy was used to warn entire nations about possible invasions. In Rome the government appointed public augurs or soothsayers to tell the future. Using heavenly signs like thunder, lightning, eclipses, and other natural phenomena as well as stones and crystals, they predicted coming events, and stayed in office as long as they were correct. The ancient Babylonians, Persians, and Chinese all used stones, crystals, and crystal balls to see into the future. Scrying into jewels, crystals, and crystal balls was also practiced by both the ancient Hindus and Egyptians. Hindu seers and holy men used to gaze into small crystal balls mounted on finger rings to develop the one-pointed concentration it took for meditation. Because clear quartz was most often associated with gazing and "seeing your way" in ancient Egypt, round, eye-shaped crystals were placed in sarcophagi and used as the eyes of the statues. The ancient Hebrews, in the New Testament (Revelations, verses 21 and 22), described the walls of the City of Jerusalem coming down from God as being made of various jewels that were "clear as crystal" and referred to clear crystal as representing the unending, all-knowing light of God, of which all the saved would partake.

☺

EARLY EUROPEAN DIVINATION AND
CRYSTAL BALL GAZING

Scrying was common among the early Celtic priests and priestesses, midwives, and healers. However, with the coming of the Christian era in the West, the practice fell into disrepute. The church fathers regarded it as a holdover from the pagan ways, and even if they didn't ban it outright, they were highly suspicious of it. In spite of the church disfavor that forced gazers underground, there were a few who, for various reasons, were quite visible. Nostradamus, the French physician and prophet who lived from 1503 to 1566, used both water and crystal balls to make more than a thousand predictions of future events that included the Napoleonic Wars, the Third Reich, the American Revolution and Civil War, and even the assassinations of presidents Lincoln and Kennedy. Dr. John Dee, the adviser and astrologer to Queen Elizabeth I of England, used his crystal ball "shew stone" to make the many accurate predictions that Queen Elizabeth relied upon to guide the British Empire. The most dramatic were his warning the queen about a plot by Spanish agents to burn the forests of England and foreseeing the attack of the Spanish Armada in 1588, which enabled the English forces to prepare for and defeat them. Count Alessandro di Cagliostro, along with his wife, was an enormously popular Italian psychic who traveled throughout Europe and the Mediterranean area working with crystal balls, channeling spirits, and engaging in psychic healing. His predictions were so accurate that even after his death his legend lived on for years, with sightings of him in Russia, Europe, and even America.

WIZARDS, MAGICIANS, AND WITCHES

Magicians, witches, and wizards, originally known as sages, wise ones, or those able to access spirits and other realities, were originally highly respected. They were most often the priests and priestesses, healers, herbalists, astrologers, and midwives and fulfilled an important function in society. The use of crystal balls by these wise ones was common among them, often accompanied by elaborate instructions for their use. Starting in the Middle Ages, as the plague killed off a large part of the population and vast social and political changes took place, anything and everyone associated with something even vaguely strange or different from the "normal" church-defined ways of living and understanding the world became objectionable and "unclean," heretical and dangerous. Wizards, witches, and magicians, then, were necessary targets because they pulled the minds and hearts away from the Catholic Church of the time, reminding people of the old earth-based ways that had offered solace and a way of living for centuries. As a result, most crystal ball readers, whether wizard, healer, or common person, went into hiding. Crystal ball gazers were careful to let no dangerous stories of their work pass beyond their walls. Their knowledge and techniques were passed down quietly from parent to child or teacher to student, often with elaborate preparatory rituals that weeded out the insincere, the talkative, and the weak. Only recently has this information about working with crystal balls been accessible to anyone but the initiated.

GYPSIES

Other than witches or wizards, Gypsies come most often to mind when we think of crystal ball gazing. Because of their nomadic

ways and alienation from mainstream European culture, the Gypsies developed their own folklore, lifestyle, and way of living. Part
of that way involved the reading of crystal balls. Gypsy women
were known as excellent crystal ball readers, their skills passed
down from mother to daughter. Because the Gypsy point of view
was so at odds with the church, Gypsies were persecuted before
the Inquisition and long afterward. Crystal ball reading served as
one form of self-protection. Whether by actual reading or trickery,
a Gypsy woman could, in the course of her reading, skillfully elicit
enough important information about the political climate in town
so she would be able to tell her band whether it was safe to stay or
if they should quickly move on. Since Gypsies were thought to be
sorcerers with the ability to heal and see into the future, people
would be intrigued and attracted to them, offering them shelter in
spite of possible repercussions.

◉

MODERN TIMES

But it wasn't until the Victorian era that scrying and divining
became accepted. During this time it wasn't unusual to see women
huddled over tea leaves, coffee grounds, cards, palms, and crystal
balls . . . often in the garb of the Gypsy woman. This practice provided an acceptable outlet from the stultifying culture of the time.
The next time that we see interest in crystal balls is at the turn of
the century, as the spiritualist movement became active. When
before crystal ball gazing and other forms of divination had been
an exotic curiosity and a cultural outlet, now they were tied to a
spiritual questing. For a brief span, and for the first time ever, crystal ball techniques began to be more available not only to a "spiritual elite," but to the everyday person. As the spiritualist
movement died down, so did the interest in crystal ball gazing. Up
until the forties in this country, psychic readings still enjoyed some

popularity, though not to the extent they had in the early 1900s. The number of psychics dwindled, and rather than being a respected parlor pastime, psychism began to be again considered strange and exotic.

Today we are experiencing a worldwide renaissance of the ancient ways, increasingly supported by science, which is beginning to change the consciousness of our culture. Though our modern culture still predominantly relies on rational models of reality and tends to disparage psychism and intuitive ways of knowing as being unproven superstition, even science is beginning to accept other forms of consciousness and their impact on all areas of our life. Visualization is known to positively affect health. The positive effects of working with color, sound, crystals, and stones is starting to be investigated by some of the most forward-thinking scientists. The power of prayer has been scientifically illustrated. New theories of time and matter, long experienced by psychics, diviners, mystics, and crystal ball gazers, are beginning to form whole areas of scientific investigation. Added to this, with the advent of the human-potential, spiritual, and New Age movements, people are beginning to accept that there are other ways of knowing than through our rational minds and that there are realities other than the standard variety. Again, divination is popular. Not only are we interested in another way of knowing, but just as in the most ancient of times, we want to know what the future holds.

2

Types of Crystal Balls

"Each phenomenon on earth is an allegory, and each allegory is an open gate through which the soul, if it is ready, can pass into the interior of the world where you and I and day and night are all one."

HERMANN HESSE

When most people think about crystal balls, the picture that comes to mind is of the clear sphere. However, there are many types of crystal ball: rock quartz; laboratory-grown quartz and glass; spheres with veils, inclusions, rainbows, and pyramids; colored stone; rutilated and mineral included. Each of these types has something special to offer. Before choosing your crystal ball, it's good to know something about these various types so you can make an educated choice. You may find that you want more than one type of crystal ball, using each one differently depending on its particular attribute. For example, you may use one sphere when you need to be more relaxed and another when you want to diagnose an illness or find a lost object.

I have many crystal balls that I place around my home purely for their beauty. I have other crystal balls that I set around my home in key places in order to energize the rooms in certain ways. Some of these spheres are natural, others are lab-grown quartz. I keep some small clear and colored stone crystal balls near my desk at work and in my workplace at home just to use as concentration tools. Anytime that I feel that I need energy, help in focusing, or need to see a larger perspective, I pick up one of these crystal balls to hold. I also have both crystal ball pendants and earrings that I wear for their energy. I occasionally look into these spheres, seeing what they "have to say," but I do most of my readings with two large natural-quartz crystal balls, one bright and the other slightly smoky.

QUARTZ CRYSTAL BALLS

There are three kinds of clear crystal balls: those made from natural-quartz crystal, laboratory-grown crystal, and glass. I recommend using either a natural-quartz crystal ball or a lab-grown sphere, not a glass sphere. Following is a description of each of these spheres and a discussion of its energetic properties and how they can help you in your reading.

Natural-quartz crystals, often referred to in ancient tradition as "veins of the earth," "frozen water," or "frozen light," were formed naturally from the elements silicon and water through millions of years of heat and pressure. Natural-quartz crystal balls are formed from these ancient quartz crystals. Carving and polishing the stones into spheres made them most powerful not only because you could see into them better, but because it was believed that the spherical shape would effortlessly draw your undivided attention. It became the perfect meditation and "seeing" tool. Whether they are shaped by hand tool or machine, most crystal balls are cut out of the crystal itself and then polished. People who cut the sphere from the crystal first find a place in the crystal that is clear and/or has something interesting inside of it that will make a good crystal ball. Then they cut around that area to form the sphere. In order to create a crystal ball, the quartz crystal that it is shaped from needs to be many times larger than the finished sphere. The reason, then, that large natural-quartz crystal balls are relatively so few is that there are not very many natural crystals that are both large and clear enough to make a large ball. (This is also why they are expensive!)

Sometimes instead of the sphere's being cut from the crystal, the entire crystal is sanded down by hand and laboriously polished away until it is in a somewhat round shape. You usually find this only in more primitive societies, dating from more ancient times. These spheres are special because the shock of having been cut is not stored within them. However, they are generally not perfectly spherical, which makes them harder to read. The harshness of the cutting in a cut crystal ball can be cleared using some of the methods explained throughout this book.

When we gaze into the quartz crystal ball, whether it is natural or grown in the laboratory, we are making use of these special energetic properties of quartz to help us focus, to feel calm, centered, and energized. It serves as a useful tool in other ways also. Your quartz crystal ball will generate negative ions in any environment in which you place it, creating a feeling of refreshment, uplift, and harmony. Also, energy, in the form of vibration, is projected from each crystal to form a field around it. This is often referred to as the "power" of the crystal. The more powerful your crystal ball, the more powerful your readings. Of course, it's not only the quartz crystal that's going to help you be more effective, but also your ability to concentrate and harmonize yourself with your sphere. Generally speaking, a larger stone can store and process more information and is more powerful. Size, however, is not the only thing affecting the power of your crystal ball. Each projected vibrational field varies in dimension not only with the size of the sphere, but also with its clarity and brilliance. All of these figure in the crystal ball's power.

When a stone has been formed to a sphere, it creates a spherical energy field with a whirlpool effect that tends to pull you in toward its center. You've probably noticed the water whirling down your drain after you take the stopper out. It's much like that. Your attention is inexorably drawn into the sphere like the water going down the drain. When you work with a sphere formed from a quartz crystal this process is amplified, deepened, and quickened because you are being influenced by its highly energetic vibrational rate. The whirlpool effect is immeasurably stronger, making it easier to narrow your attention to one point, something that you need to do in order to "read" your crystal ball. This is true whether you are working with a natural-quartz crystal ball or a laboratory-grown quartz crystal ball.

You can raise your vibration still further if you take the time to harmonize yourself with the quartz crystal. As your vibration rises, your energy automatically rises from your lower survival- and power-oriented energy centers to your higher, more psychic- and spiritual-energy centers. When this happens you automatically find your heart opening, your intuition increasing, and your awareness extending. Eventually, it becomes effortless to enter a trance state and hear your "inner voice." You begin to operate from higher levels of consciousness. Shamans refer to this phenomenon as being more in touch with the spirit world. It is in this state, say the ancestors, when we can "hear the stone people talking" and can "talk" with them. Your interaction with your quartz sphere can begin to open you up this way. That is why the old teachers used to refer to crystal balls as gateways or doorways to the beyond and to the inner self. Because of the tendency of the quartz crystal to help you open in this way, when you use a quartz crystal ball your reading is going to be infinitely deeper and more meaningful than if you use glass.

☙

HOLDING OR WEARING CLEAR CRYSTAL BALLS

Clear crystal balls are not only good for gazing but can also be held or worn to give you energy and to open any chakra or subtle energy center. A clear 34- to 40-millimeter (about a 1 ¼-inch to 1 ¾-inch diameter) ball can be used as a charging sphere. This will help amplify the clarity of your readings and give you the energy to hold your concentration one-pointedly for a long time. A clear crystal charging sphere held in your right hand will not only lend you its energetic and amplifying capabilities but will help you "send" your questions and intentions into the gazing sphere. Held in the left hand, it will help you "receive" answers, guidance, and anything else that there is to be received from the reading.

Clear crystal spheres can be worn over any energy center to activate and open it to help you with your reading and with your own personal unfoldment. An 18-millimeter (about ¾" to 1") sphere is a good size to wear between your abdomen and heart center. Worn here it will both strengthen your will, enabling you to maintain your focused intention, and help you open your heart center, the center of love, compassion, and empathy. A 12- or 14-millimeter sphere (marble-sized) is good to wear over the throat center, the center of communication and spiritual attunement. An 8-millimeter sphere (between ¼" and ½" diameter) is a good size for earrings. Clear spheres worn on or around the ears will work on opening your third eye, the center of intuition and psychic awareness and to some extent, your crown center, the center of "cosmic consciousness."

Use these crystal spheres to help you balance your energies and do a centered reading. If you are feeling too grounded or have a heavy, sluggish feeling, wear a crystal sphere near one of your upper energy centers. Likewise, if your mind is racing or you feel shaky, nervous, or jumpy, wear your crystal sphere near your heart or even as low as near your navel point.

☻

VEILS, INCLUSIONS, PHANTOMS, AND RAINBOWS

Many crystal gazers prefer natural quartz because it is usually filled with veils and inclusions that provide both beauty and help for your reading. Veils are what look like wispy clouds inside your sphere. Inclusions look like cracks or fracturing inside the stone. While you're gazing, you might find veils or inclusions that resemble doorways you can pass through. Sometimes they resemble inner landscapes through which you can travel deeper into the ball. This landscape effect is even more pronounced in a special class of crystal balls that have colored mineral deposits. For example, green-chlorite-included crystal looks as if it's filled with forests and mountains. Many times in my reading I find what looks like a pathway through this landscape and follow it to go deeper into the ball or deeper into my trance state. You can gaze at these inner landscapes and find that they suggest pictures or scenes to have a particular meaning for the reading.

Some of these internal fractures or inclusions create rainbows in your crystal ball. Not only do these rainbows add a special beauty to your crystal sphere, but you can use them to travel into the heavens or into the astral planes of consciousness. Just keep gazing into the rainbows until you can visualize traveling through their sparkling light into these higher realms.

One of the most highly prized of the mineral-included quartz crystal spheres is called rutilated quartz. Rutiles look like very slender copper, brown, black, or gold needles inside the crystal. They are actually very slender crystals naturally occurring within the larger. As you look into your crystal ball you can use these needle formations to suggest pictures to you and read them much as you would read tea leaves or coffee grounds. I'll talk more about this process of interpreting the pictures suggested by inclusions later in the chapter about interpreting your readings.

Phantoms are also very special. They resemble pyramids within your quartz sphere. That pyramid effect is created when a crystal stops growing and is capped by another one over its surface. You may see a sphere where there are several pyramids each on top of the other. Crystal workers find these pyramids good for sending messages, feelings, thoughts, or healing, or for projecting oneself out into space or into the inner worlds. If you want to send a message or anything else using the pyramid inside your crystal ball, do this: Gaze into your crystal ball and visualize yourself moving inside the pyramid. Look upward toward its tip above you and send your message out through it to the person or place that you intend. Then visualize yourself leaving the pyramid and either continuing with your gazing or backing out of the crystal ball to end your reading.

◉

LABORATORY-GROWN QUARTZ CRYSTAL BALLS

Laboratory-grown quartz crystals are "raised" for their easily manipulated, high rate of vibration. Initially used by the computer and electronics industry, they have the amplifying qualities of natural quartz. Because they are grown in a controlled manner that you'd never find in nature, they are all perfectly clear and very bright, with no veils or inclusions. (Sometimes if the ball has been cracked, you can use these cracks as inclusions.) Lab-grown crystal balls are formed from lab-grown quartz. They are very beautiful. People who read these crystal balls prefer their clarity to veils, inclusions, and other inner markings, which they find distracting. They experience the clear sphere as helping one enter the Zenlike clear-mind state from which the most pure trance sensations come. The clear sphere suggests boundless space or infinity.

Some crystal workers believe that all natural-quartz crystal balls are stronger than lab-grown quartz spheres. However, in my experience, though a natural-quartz crystal ball will tend to be stronger, not all of them are. Ultimately you have to check each crystal ball and see for yourself. As you may imagine, it is very rare to find an optically clear sphere, especially if it is large. If you do find one, it is the most expensive of all the clear crystal balls. The nice thing about a lab-grown quartz ball is that you can get a clear one for far less than the price of a natural-quartz ball of the same size, even one that is highly included.

CRYSTALS AND STONES—OUR OLDEST ANCESTORS

Native Americans call crystals and other rocks "stone people" and regard them respectfully as our "oldest ancestors." As our oldest ancestors, all stones have something to teach us if we know how to listen. According to ancient legend, quartz crystals were thought of as being storehouses of our planetary history, the millions of years of earth formation recorded vibrationally, locked within each crystal during its creation and growth. The teachings also say that all quartz crystals are energetically connected with each other. These interconnected "veins" form energetic pathways carrying life force throughout the planet as our veins carry blood in our body. It was believed that these energetic pathways and informational repositories could be used to connect us with each other, with all of the earth's elements, plants, animals, and minerals and the entire solar system. When we use a natural-quartz crystal ball, we are connecting with our most ancient of ancestors, and if we listen to "voices" that come through our crystal ball we can gain much wisdom. Not only that, but some traditions add that ancient wise ones or special teachers programmed special teachings into some crystals and crystal balls to be found by those who would follow later. Some legends speak of some of these special teachers entering into the crystals at their death in order to pass their learning to those who would receive the crystal later.

A lab-grown quartz is stone, but instead of being a stone ancestor, it is more like a stone child. It is very young and new to our planet. Though we can use its amplification and energetic properties, it has a limited amount to teach us. For these reasons some crystal ball gazers feel that the natural-quartz crystal ball is preferable to the lab-grown crystal ball. I have both natural and lab-grown crystal balls. Sometimes people begin with a lab-grown ball because they find it easier to start gazing in a larger sphere and the large-sized lab-grown crystal ball is much less expensive than its natural counterpart. Try them both and see what you experience.

GLASS SPHERES

A glass sphere, made from blown glass instead of rock, has none of the vibrational qualities of lab-grown or natural-quartz crystal and so is much harder to read. It doesn't store information or amplify like quartz, so it has no history and, other than its shape, offers no help for your reading. I would recommend that you at least get a quartz sphere. If you can't tell whether a crystal ball is glass or quartz, ask the person helping at the store. He or she should also know whether the ball is lab-grown or natural. Sometimes you can see a seam in a glass ball. If all else fails, you can tell by the price. A glass ball is going to be significantly less expensive than quartz.

BRIGHTNESS AND STRENGTH

Generally speaking, the brighter a crystal ball is, the more powerful it is. By brighter I don't mean that it sparkles, although some very bright crystals seem to sparkle. You can get a sense of what I mean by "brightness" by thinking of the difference between a new white shirt and an old one that's been washed many times: The old one looks kind of dull. It even feels dull. They're both white, but the new white shirt looks and feels brighter. Clear crystal balls are like that. If you compare two or more spheres to each other you'll see that one appears brighter than the other.

Natural-quartz crystal balls vary from bright to cloudy to dull. A lab-grown crystal ball is almost always very bright. That is one advantage it has over the natural-quartz crystal ball, which varies in terms of brightness. Sometimes a very bright lab-grown crystal ball is energetically stronger than a dull natural-quartz crystal sphere. Usually you can get a strong intuitive sense of the crystal ball's strength by picking it up or even just by looking at it. If you have been working with quartz crystals for a while, you can physically feel this vibration. It's a buzzing sensation or a slight wind in your hand. If the crystal ball is especially strong you can feel this buzzing sensation go from your hands clear up your arms and even through your body.

COLORED STONE SPHERES

Clear-quartz crystal balls are not the only ones that can be used for scrying work, even if they are the most common. Any translucent colored stone can also be used. Throughout history people have also used opaque stones like pyrite, hematite, obsidian, and black onyx. Because these are solid rather than see-through, people read the patterns of light and shadow on their reflective surfaces much as if using a mirror. They would use the surface to help them clear their minds and enter a trance state, moving past the limitations of their rational thinking patterns.

It has been well established that color has an effect on our thoughts and feelings. Color is used in therapy and healing. Different colors not only evoke certain emotional and psychological reactions but have cultural associations as well. The same is true of colored stones. Colored stones can affect you physically, emotionally, and mentally and can help balance and energize your subtle energy system. They also can affect the environment in which they are placed. This automatic process can be amplified when you use your focused will to intend it to happen. When you use colored stones and crystals in healing and other work, you learn that you need to be sensitive not only to the color of the stone but to its density as well. As with clear-quartz crystal balls, the degree of opacity, brilliance, and clarity are important. Generally speaking, the clearer the stone, the more etheric is its quality. This is true no matter what color it is. An opaque stone sphere has a more dense, grounding quality. In other words, an emerald has a lighter or more etheric quality than African green malachite. Both of these green colors are good for opening the heart to love. However, the emerald might turn your thoughts to the love of the higher spirit, while the malachite might connect you with the nurturing love of our mother earth. Each color has a sense of a different degree of coolness or heat. Some colors feel harsher or more abrasive in quality, while others are more soothing and subtle. A bright red garnet, for example, is activating, while a light blue celestite is gently cooling and calming. Each colored stone sphere also has a subtle difference, even if it is the same type or color as another. There will be an energetic difference between two spheres that are the same yellow color of citrine, for example. One citrine may feel more like energizing fire while the other may feel like gentle sunlight. These subtle differences cannot be seen, only sensed. The best way to do it is to hold the sphere between your two hands, harmonize yourself with it, enter a meditative state, and see what comes to your attention. One or the other will be more favorable for your intended use. In my other crystal book, *The Complete Crystal Guidebook*, there is a complete colored-stone chart to help you to learn more about their use. At the end of this book I have also listed other books that you may want to refer to.

There are many ways to use colored stones and spheres. I'll talk about a few of them as well as some of the best colored stone spheres to use. Some of the colored stone spheres are good for gazing. The best ones are clear enough to see into. Some stones, while they would be lovely to gaze into, are prohibitively expensive in a size large enough to be a gazing sphere. I recommend that you start with a clear-quartz sphere, because it is the best all-around to use and, as I said before, the easiest to see into. You can place different-colored spheres around your environment to charge it with special color in order to create a certain feeling. For example, I have a rose-quartz sphere near where I sleep to introduce the quality of love and peace. When you work with stone healing you might use a small colored sphere to rub over your body or that part of your body that needs the energy of that color.

❂

COLORED STONE CHARGING SPHERES

After starting with a clear quartz you may find that you are drawn to use one color or another to balance yourself in your reading. Holding a colored stone sphere in your left hand as a charging sphere while you read will influence your body, thoughts, and feelings with its color. If you're lacking vitality, for example, you might hold a yellow citrine sphere. You may need a color for grounding if you're feeling shaky or nervous. If you're having trouble hearing your "intuitive voice," for example, you might need another for bringing you further up in your higher energy centers. Not only can you hold a colored stone charging sphere to influence yourself, but you can also use it to program your clear-quartz sphere with its color. To do this, hold the colored stone sphere up near the clear gazing sphere. Then visualize the color flowing from the colored charging sphere into the clear sphere. When you do this with enough concentration, your clear gazing sphere will take on the characteristics of the color with which you charged it. When you're through with your reading, don't forget to clear the color out of your clear sphere. (The next chapter will give you more detail about programming and clearing crystal balls.)

To help you, here are some of the most popular colors other than clear quartz that you may want to add to your crystal ball collection. Not only are these some of the most popular alternative colors, but they aren't prohibitively expensive.

☺

SMOKY QUARTZ: THE GROUNDING
AND CALMING STONE

Some natural-crystal balls are slightly brown. These crystal spheres should not be mistaken for being dull quartz. They are called smoky quartz and rather than being devalued, they are prized for their grounding and calming capabilities. (A smoky quartz can have a brighter feeling than a dull clear quartz. You have to pick it up or touch it and see what kind of intuitive feeling you get.) Some smoky quartz is just a light shade of brown, so light that if you didn't hold it against a white backdrop, you wouldn't see it. At the other extreme, some smoky quartz is so dark as to be almost black. The dark smokies are very grounding, but hard to see into. I'd recommend using a lighter shade so that you can take advantage of both the clarity and grounding capabilities of the crystal. One of my two favorite crystal balls is a light shade of smoky quartz.

Sometimes people read from a larger clear-quartz sphere and hold a hand-sized smoky quartz in their left hand as a grounding rod. The darker the sphere is, the deeper your grounding. The round shape of the sphere also has a gentling effect on you while you hold it. The smaller smoky ball in your left hand will bring calming and grounding to you. (Other stone spheres that are good to use for this type of grounding are black agate and black onyx.) If you find it distracting to hold the sphere while you read, wear it as a pendant below your heart center near your abdomen. Don't wear it as low as your navel, because that may ground you too much. It helps to strengthen your nervous system and to ground and calm yourself not only during your readings, but anytime that you feel high-strung, anxious, or tense. This is an especially good way to balance any crystal spheres worn on your upper energy centers, like earrings.

Occasionally during your readings you can get off balance, too "high," unable to verbalize the images that you're seeing in the reading. It's a feeling of not quite being able to pull them down from the sky. If that happens, hold your smoky quartz and visualize yourself as being a tree extending your branches high in the sky and your roots deep into the earth. In order to send your branches into the sky you need deep roots. Feel yourself balanced between the sky and the deep earth. Then visualize these images that you want to communicate floating up in the sky. Imagine yourself pulling them gently down from the sky, through your branches, the top of your head, down your trunk, through your heart, down your legs and out your feet, through your roots into mother earth. If you visualize this strongly enough, you'll be able to find the words to describe your vision. Using a smoky quartz will give you these "roots," connecting you with the stabilizing qualities of mother earth.

Sometimes you can get the shakes during your readings. I remember that happening to me. For a while, when I would meditate or do readings, my entire body would start shaking, my neck would get tight, and my jaw would clench. A yoga teacher that I had at the time instructed me to do two hours a day of one navel-point yoga exercise for a year to strengthen me. He said that it was necessary so that my subtle and physical nervous system could handle what I was experiencing through my "third eye" and my crown chakra (energy center). I found that wearing a smoky-quartz sphere between my belly button and heart center helped.

As with any setting, keep it as open as possible so that light can go through the ball, continually charging it with energy. The sphere is best left undrilled because that may interfere with its energy flow. It is best to wear a smoky-quartz ball of sufficient size to have enough power. An 18-millimeter or approximately 1" diameter sphere is a good size for a pendant.

◉

CHINESE FLUORITE: HEART, HEALING, AND SPIRIT

This is a colorful, see-through crystal found in Canada, Italy, Mexico, England, and other places throughout the world. The colors range from clear opaque to yellow, black, pink, green, and purple. This crystal is not from the quartz family. Its crystals are shaped as cubes, octahedrons, and dodecahedrons. When they are cut into sphere shapes they don't have the same vibrational qualities of quartz that will help your gazing, but they are very pretty. The problem with them is that they are somewhat soft and can scratch or break easily, so you have to handle or wear them carefully. Some fluorite is dark or somewhat opaque and so isn't clear enough to gaze into with any effectiveness. Other fluorite, particularly some of the Chinese fluorite, is more translucent. Chinese fluorite spheres are a mixture of purple and green banded together. Purple is known for channeling in spiritual and feminine energy. It's good for calming and any kind of healing—spiritual, mental, emotional, and physical. Green brings in the nurturing, feminine energy of our mother earth. It is also associated with the physical healing of the heart and those heart qualities of compassion and love. Fluorite will bring a gentle, healing quality to your readings and would be excellent for any readings that are for diagnosing any kind of illness. A fluorite sphere placed in the environment, whether it's in your home or office desk, will tend to create those same feelings around you. There will be a sense of gentle nurturing, peace and loving expansiveness.

If you hold a fluorite quartz in your left hand while you read a larger clear crystal quartz, it will help you to keep your heart open both to the other person and to the higher spirit. It will help you to channel in the feminine, healing spiritual force. Generally speaking, a larger stone can store and process more information and is more powerful, but you would want a sphere that fits comfortably in your hand. Depending on the size of your hands, a 34- to 40-millimeter or approximately 1 ¼" to 1 ¾" sphere is a good size for this. If you hold the Chinese fluorite in your right hand it will help you be more gentle and nurturing in the deliverance of your reading for someone else. Holding it in your right hand will help you send a feeling of peace into the other as you do your reading. When diagnosing and working with illness I'd hold the Chinese fluorite in my left hand while gazing into a clear sphere. If you are holding a Chinese fluorite instead of gazing into it, you don't need to have a see-through stone. Look for one with nice color with a balance of green to purple that appeals to you.

A Chinese fluorite sphere can also be worn around your neck if you don't want to hold one during your readings. Wear it near your heart center in the middle of your chest. A 24" chain or cord usually is a good length for women, slightly longer for men. Wearing it will tend to bring to you the same kinds of energies that you'll experience while holding it; healing, peace, nurturing and spiritual insight. As with the smoky-quartz sphere, an 18-millimeter or 1" diameter size is good to wear. As with any crystal, be sure that it's mounted undrilled in a setting that lets lots of light through the sphere to charge it up. The same basics about color and opacity apply to the "wearing sphere" as with the "holding sphere," since you're not gazing into it. Hold it over your heart center, close your eyes, get centered, and see what it feels like to you.

☺

AMETHYST: THE SPIRITUAL AND HEALING STONE

Amethyst is from the quartz family and is known for both its healing properties and its ability to channel in the violet ray of the highest spirituality. There is cape amethyst from Africa as well as large (though dwindling) quantities in Mexico and Brazil. Amethyst is an amazingly versatile stone. It's often associated with the moon, with feminine energy, creativity, and intuition. It is very calming. Not only can it stimulate psychic abilities, but it can also open you to the highest worlds of the spiritual. It puts us in touch with "cosmic consciousness" and leads us into the energy centers of the crown chakra and those above the crown. Amethyst is good for any kind of healing: mental, emotional, spiritual, psychic, and physical. It will help to lessen pain. If you're working to heal something and don't know what stone to use, try an amethyst. Amethyst will work with healing and calming in every way that purple fluorite will, but amethyst is stronger.

Amethyst crystal balls that you can gaze into are more expensive than both lab-grown and natural quartz. They are even more expensive in the larger sizes, since a big see-through amethyst is relatively rare. Because of the price and rarity, people who want an amethyst sphere to gaze into will choose a smaller one, perhaps from 40 to 50 millimeters (about a 3" diameter). The problem is that amethyst is already harder to gaze into than clear quartz because of its lack of clarity and the density of the color, so getting a smaller amethyst gazing sphere only compounds the problem. Some crystal ball gazers use an amethyst only if they are doing a reading for healing purposes. Others use the large clear sphere and direct their focused intention to program it with the violet color so that it "acts" like an amethyst. More often than not, you can use the method of holding an amethyst charging sphere in your hand as you read from the larger clear gazing sphere. As always, hold the charging sphere in your left hand if you want to receive and in your right hand if you want to send or project an intention into the gazing sphere.

As with the other stones, 18-millimeter (1" diameter) amethyst spheres worn near your heart center and 12- or 14-millimeter (approximately ½") spheres near your throat center are good sizes to wear. If you want to wear them on or near your ears to open your third eye, relax your head, jaw, neck, shoulders, and head, or help open your crown center, 8-millimeter spheres are a good size. (I sometimes like to wear larger sizes, but they do get in the way.) The 8-millimeter spheres are large enough to have an effect and are also small enough to be worn day in and day out.

☺

ROSE QUARTZ: THE LOVE STONE

Rose quartz is associated with the energy center in the middle of your chest . . . your heart center. Rose quartz doesn't have much to do with the organ itself, although it can help calm a racing pulse. It has more to do with your emotions and those qualities of compassion and empathy. Rose quartz will help energize and open you to the wisdom, ecstasy, and equanimity of your open heart. This stone is used to help you be vulnerable, to let down your distance from people, to feel safe. Carry this vulnerability and resultant strength into your reading. Rose quartz even feels soft, though it's a hard stone. It feels like a baby rabbit, or young fawn. Ah-h-h-h-h . . . is the sound of the open heart and of rose quartz. It's the sigh of surrender, of letting go. Whenever you find the need for forgiveness in your readings, you can use rose quartz. If you want your readings to reflect real wisdom, use both your psychic vision and the wisdom of your heart. When you use rose quartz to open your heart center you become privy to an endless river of wisdom that goes far beyond intellectualism and psychicism. You are able to see the deeper meanings that support the events of your life, and with your heart open you experience people more deeply.

Use rose quartz anytime that you want to soften or gentle something or someone. Use it to soothe and lift depression. If your clear sphere seems to fill with darkness or what seem like gray clouds, hold a rose quartz and imagine it gently penetrating and lifting the darkness. Sometimes in reading you'll come upon something that feels dark or scary, as if it's forbidden territory. If you're reading for someone else, it may be that you have approached memories that he or she had repressed and is scared of releasing. It may be something traumatic or very sad. Hold or wear your rose-quartz sphere and imagine that the trauma or old wound that is obscuring the vision lifts and reveals what it was hiding. Imagine that the pink of the rose-quartz sphere surrounds what is holding the heart closed in fear and is gently releasing and revealing what is hidden. If it is something that you are seeing in the crystal ball, or not quite seeing because of your own personal fears or resistance, hold your rose-quartz sphere in your hand or wear it over your heart center to calm your fears and to gently gain you entry to the vision.

Almost all rose-quartz spheres are opaque. Occasionally I encounter one that is see-through, and I myself have a totally clear rose quartz that I use for healing work. Most rose quartz, however, you can't see through or inside of, so they don't work as gazing stones. Instead use rose quartz as charging spheres, holding them in your hands or wearing them as pendants or earrings. If you use a rose-quartz sphere for gazing, be aware that it can have a tendency to make you become so emotional that you can't see beyond your emotions, especially if you are tired. I would recommend balancing yourself with other stones in both the upper and lower energy centers.

☾

THE SUNSHINE STONES: YELLOW CITRINE, TOPAZ, AMETRINE, AND AMBER

Think of the sun, of its warmth, of its fire and of its light. Throughout history and myth the sun has been thought of as the "life giver" . . . as father sun to mother moon. The sun grows, nourishes, and empowers. With its golden rays, all life grows strong and flourishes. This power of the sun is what is represented by all yellow stones, each in its special way. A yellow sphere held in your hand or worn while you do your reading will charge that reading with sunlight. It might be used to reveal the brighter side of a problem. Or, if you're growing tired, its solar flares can charge you with energy. Yellow is the color of the navel point, the energy center near your belly button. Among other things, this is the seat of the will and of inner strength. It also has to do with nervous strength, with both your physical and subtle nervous system. Besides grounding yourself by holding or wearing a black agate, onyx, or smoky quartz, you can use a yellow stone. Yellow tiger eye, an iridescent yellow-and-brown stone, can charge you with sun qualities as well as ground you.

Yellow citrine is very light in feeling as well as being solar in quality. Using yellow citrine will not only help strengthen you but will help lighten you up as well. Anything that comes up in your reading that needs dispersing can be helped by yellow citrine as well as by aqua aura or aquamarine. Yellow topaz is another stone that has both sky and sun qualities. I used to have a large topaz crystal that I could use for gazing. Both yellow citrine and topaz, especially in sizes large enough to make a gazing sphere, are rare and therefore quite expensive. If you were attracted to these stones, you'd probably want to have them as smaller spheres that you wore or used as charging spheres.

Ametrine is a highly prized mixture of both amethyst and yellow citrine. The colors are layered tones of healing amethyst and life-giving yellow citrine. In places the two colors blend together for a bit as they change from one to another. That blending has a smoky feeling and adds grounding qualities to the stone. Sometimes crystal ball readers like to use ametrine in order to join spiritual realities with earth realities. If you have a client, for example, who can't experience the spiritual realities because he or she is so mired in the overwhelming press of everyday problems, ametrine will help be your bridge.

Amber varies from totally opaque and cream-colored to a clear amber or yellow. You can gaze into amber, if the sphere is large enough. A large sphere in amber, however, would be prohibitively expensive, especially if it was natural rather than pressed or reconstituted. As with yellow citrine and topaz, it is best to use amber as a hand-held sphere or as jewelry. Amber has the fire, yet it is calmer and more nurturing. Unlike yellow citrine and topaz, which tend to be more "male" in their energy, amber was traditionally known as a woman's stone or representative of the life-giving energy of the goddess. It was used for childbirth and pregnancy. Using amber, you can not only energize, but help birth any event, any way of thinking or feeling. It helps stimulate any kind of transformation. The ancients believed that because it was formed from the sap of trees, amber was of the nature spirits, especially of the tree spirits with their branches so high in the sun, bringing life force through its body down through its roots.

If you wear amber spheres, it will help strengthen you to wear one near your third chakra, around your waist, dropping about two inches below your navel. Most people who do this wear the sphere on a cord under their clothing so as not to be conspicuous. (You may not like the attention.) I used to do this anytime I was going to be in a situation where I needed extra willpower, or when I felt that my nervous system needed strengthening. If you wear an amber sphere pendant, it's strongest to wear it below your heart center. Of course, there are no hard-and-fast rules. You may find that you intuitively feel you should wear your amber sphere over your heart center in order to "warm your heart." This is good in your reading if you find that it's becoming too mental or too intellectual and you're not getting to the center of an issue. Use amber to warm your heart so it opens as gently as a flower unfolds its petals to the sun. Warming your heart will help draw you away from or balance yourself with the "colder" mental energies. As with all of the spheres that you wear, 18 millimeter are good pendant sizes, 12 to 14 millimeter are good for throat-center pendants and some drop earrings, and 8 millimeter are good for all drop earrings and earposts.

☾

THE SKY STONES: AQUA AURA, BLUE TOPAZ, TURQUOISE, BLUE CALCITE, AND LIGHT BLUE FLUORITE

Because of their lightness and heavenly colors, the "sky stones" are very good for "lightening up" anything—physically, mentally, and emotionally. Use sky-stone spheres to help you uncoil the tight knot of anger, lift the heavy feeling of depression, and release you from unhappiness. These stone spheres are good for dispersing anything stuck in your reading and will help rescue your reading if it bogs down or goes in circles. They will also help bring your energy up from the lower to the higher chakras. If you're feeling so overwhelmed in a highly emotional reading that you lose your way, the sky stones are good for recovering your balance. For example, if you're feeling so sad about a situation you're seeing in the crystal ball that you can't offer anything else to the reading, do this: Take your sky-stone pendant or holding or charging sphere in your hand, place it on your throat center, and imagine that energy rises from your heart to your throat. You can imagine this as a light blue current of light opening up and expanding your chest, calming your breathing, and relaxing your shoulders as it moves up to the center of your throat. After you've established this connection, your sadness should start lifting. Then move the sphere up to your third eye in the middle of your forehead and imagine the energy moving up from your throat out of your third eye. Feel or imagine the column of blue light open from your heart to your third eye. (This entire process can be done with only a few breaths when you're practiced.) As you hold the sky blue sphere in your left hand again or let the pendant rest in its original position, carry this rebalanced feeling within you. You may feel the sadness again, but it will be evened out with the insight of higher vision . . . as will the rest of your reading.

All of these light blue stones are related to the energy center at your throat which, when open, helps you stay allied with the higher spirit. The prayer, "Not my will but thine," fits perfectly with these stones. When you use these "sky stones" and stimulate your throat energy center, the love of your heart is joined with the intuition and spiritual vision of your third-eye and crown centers. The throat is also the energy center for all forms of communication, interpersonal and spiritual, helping you with communicating truths and visions that come from higher spirit. Because of these attributes, sky stones are of tremendous help during your reading.

According to Native American teachings, turquoise not only is related to your throat chakra but also absorbs negativity. I know one reader who always keeps a second turquoise sphere close by her when she does readings with her larger clear sphere. She feels that it will absorb any negativity that may have been stirred up during the reading.

Aqua aura, sometimes called the "angel stone," bears special mention because of both its formation and its uniqueness. Aqua aura is a clear-quartz crystal that has been electronically bonded with gold to create an aquamarine color. Because heat is used in the bonding process, a significant percentage of quartz crystal spheres will shatter. Sometimes this causes internal fractures that are quite pretty, creating rainbows and interesting inclusions that are useful in your reading. If there are too many fractures, however, they will interfere with the energetic properties of the sphere. Because of the breakage and the cost involved in the bonding process, aqua aura usually is more expensive than clear quartz and many other stones.

When I first was introduced to an aqua aura I was a bit leery, because I don't usually like treated stones. When I held it, however, it felt great. It's like a blending of gold and crystal with slightly iridescent violet overtones that are seen when the stone is turned side to side. It feels angelic. The blue color is similar to aquamarine or blue topaz. It has a very light feeling and can make you feel as if you're floating in the sky.

Aqua aura will help connect us with the angels. Whether you're gazing into an aqua-aura crystal ball, holding it, or wearing it, you can speak from your heart and ask that your angelic guide(s) come through and communicate with you. You may see them in your sphere, hear their voices in your mind, feel them in your body, or sense them around you. Their communications have many voices, their language is prayer and their pathway is your heart.

Most of these sky stones are not cut into gazing balls. It's too hard to find a rough stone that's large enough to cut a sizable ball. If they're cut into spheres at all, it's usually the smaller sizes. Again, some of these may be quite costly. Turquoise, of course, you can't gaze into, but it makes a good charging sphere. Your best selection for gazing would probably be an aqua aura because it's not as expensive and is more available than aquamarine, blue topaz, or light blue fluorite. You can gaze into it easily and it won't scratch as easily as blue calcite.

A hand-held aqua-aura charging sphere should be very effective to use along with your larger clear gazing sphere. Hold your aqua-aura sphere in your right hand while you gaze into your clear crystal ball to help you disperse anything that is stuck. If you are doing your reading, for example, and you find your vision clouded, you can hold the aqua aura and imagine it dispersing the cloud until your vision is clear again. If you're having trouble finding the right words to communicate what you're seeing in your crystal ball, hold the aqua-aura sphere in either hand or, if it's small enough, over your throat center.

Wearing an aqua-aura or other sky blue sphere on an 18" or 16" length cord or chain will help open your throat center. If you are going to wear it near or on your throat center a smaller size is best, because anything larger can feel too heavy. Smaller light blue spheres are also good to wear on or near your ears. As in all sphere earposts, 8-millimeter (¼" or smaller) size is the most comfortable. Drop earrings can be larger and still be comfortable. If you wear either clear, aqua-aura, or other light blue spheres on your ears, it will tend to open your third eye, the center of intuition, creativity, and psychic awareness. At the same time it will help keep your throat center open to help you communicate what you "see." This is excellent for crystal gazing. Again, if you start feeling too "spacy" and begin to lose your grounding while you're wearing your aqua-aura earrings, place a smoky, black-agate, or onyx pendant near your abdomen, or hold a "charging" (hand-held) grounding sphere in your left hand. (If you don't want to hold the grounding stone, wear a small grounding sphere as a ring on your left hand. Some people will wear grounding spheres as rings on both hands.) This should reestablish your balance. If you're not sure if you're rebalanced, imagine yourself as a tree, branches in the sky, roots into the earth, joined in the open heart.

☺

LAPIS, SODALITE, AND DUMORTIERITE: THE PSYCHIC STONES

These stones are used to energize the third eye, the center of intuition and psychic attunement. It goes without saying that you need to at least be highly intuitive in order to do crystal ball gazing. Being able to see into the psychic planes of reality also helps. Dark or royal blue stones like lapis, dumortierite, and sodalite help develop all psychic abilities. These stone spheres can also be used to take you into the astral world. (Some of these techniques will be discussed in later chapters.) Lapis was so prized by the ancient Egyptians for this ability that it was considered sacred. It is through these stones that you can extend your consciousness to experience that what seems miraculous in the physical world actually has its own natural laws in astral and other worlds. In other words, with a larger frame of reference it all makes sense.

Lapis, sodalite, and dumortierite are not the only stone spheres that can be used to energize your third eye. Most dark blue stones can be used. Blue tourmalines and sapphires are effective. Some of the chrysacolas are useful also. Usually chrysacola is dark blue mixed with turquoise color, so it also opens your throat center and absorbs negativity.

When I first began crystal ball gazing I sometimes used to wear either a clear-quartz crystal or a lapis over my third eye. Before I began my reading, I would put my lapis or crystal headband on. Then part of my centering and harmonizing with the crystal ball would include visualizing the center of my forehead relaxing and gently opening to a ray of sapphire- or lapis-colored light. I'd feel as if a dark blue light was filling my head with every inbreath, bringing me vision and insight. I'd ground myself and center in my heart while maintaining this third-eye vision. Then I'd begin my reading.

Sometimes you can create a headband with a small 8-millimeter sphere hanging from a chain or a cord. Just get a pendant and adjust it. I used to tuck them in the brim of my hat. Clear-quartz and dark blue spheres like lapis, sodalite, dumortierite, sapphire, and dark blue tourmaline can be worn as earposts or short drop earrings.

You should be aware that if you're going to stimulate your third-eye center this intensely, you will need to be especially careful to ground yourself. (If you find that your jaw is clenching, you're shaking, or you're having trouble finding words to describe your vision, you're not grounded enough!) You might want to wear a sphere pendant over your heart center or even lower. Be sure to "plant your roots."

As with the other color stones, you can hold a charging sphere in either your left or right hand, depending on whether you are sending or receiving. Sapphire would be beautiful but prohibitively expensive and quite rare. Sodalite and dumortierite have much the same feeling as lapis, but are a touch more grounding. They are harder stones, so they won't scratch or chip as easily and make good third-eye charging spheres.

☻

THE GREEN STONES:
NURTURING, PROSPERITY, AND ABUNDANCE

Ancient tradition has always taught that earth is our mother. Without its trees, its waters, and its soil, we would have no life. Like milk from the mother to child, the earth takes care of us. Bearheart, the Native American medicine man that I worked with for so many years, used to point out that not only are we taken care of by mother earth, but so are all plants, animals, and other forms of life. As such, all other forms of life are, in a sense, our relations. As Bearheart introduced me to sweat lodges and other Native American ceremonies, I would always hear the people talk about "standing tall brothers" (trees), "brother hawk" or "grandfather eagle." Not only was this a reflection of their sense of relationship, but it also honored them as being just as important a part of the creation as we are. We are not the masters but only the relatives of everything else in creation.

Green is another color traditionally associated with your heart center. Rather than dealing with the emotional part of the heart, green stones like green aventurine, African malachite, green fluorite, green calcite, emerald, peridot, and green tourmaline are used for the nurturing part of our heart, the part that relates to mother earth and honors all creation. Crystal healers also use these green stones to take care of the physical heart. They visualize the green of the stone soothing the heart and slowing its rhythm. It's like getting a "heart massage" to relax and renew an overworked muscle. You probably won't have much use for this in your crystal ball gazing, but if you get tense or your heart starts racing, try wearing a green aventurine or African malachite sphere over your heart center or hold an aventurine charging sphere.

If in your crystal ball reading you come across anything having to do with nurturing, use a green sphere like aventurine, African malachite, tourmaline, or emerald to help. Hold a green stone charging sphere and feel as if you're being filled with nurturing energy. If there is a problem with nurturing, you can visualize your gazing ball filling with green light from your charging sphere. Then enter into the green sphere and the problem will become apparent to you as well as its solution. Once, after entering the crystal ball, I came into the presence of a woman who had sprouting from her womb all manner of plants and animals while she was in a state of pure ecstasy. I felt as if I were witnessing the birth of all life. Later, when I was thinking about the vision, I felt that it was showing me my interrelationship with all of life and that an essential joy underlies all of creation.

Proper nurturing creates growth. To grow is to prosper. As such, green stones have been used to attract prosperity since ancient times. Whenever you have issues in your reading having to do with money matters, or whether something will thrive, or a general sense of well-being, use a green sphere. Wear one over your heart center to attract these qualities to you, or use a green charging sphere to bring these energies closer to your attention. Green tourmaline is widely known by crystal healers as a transformer. Besides being useful for everything else that other green stones are, it will also help in transforming any energy state or emotion to another. It will also help you during changing life situations. If you are doing a crystal ball reading for someone who wants to know how to change a particular situation in his or her life, green tourmaline will help bring some clarity. If you don't have a green tourmaline, you can visualize your gazing sphere as if it's green tourmaline just as you did with the other colors.

Finally, green stones are good for cooling. Very often the best stones for this are the light green ones like some green aventurines, green calcite, and some green fluorite. Some stone healers use these stones to cool fevers or "put out the fire" of raging infections. In crystal ball gazing you'd use the light green stone sphere to cool off any heated situation.

☉

RED AVENTURINE: THE MANIFESTING STONE

Red aventurine is not really red, it's orange. Orange is the color that corresponds to the second chakra, the energy center near our sexual organs. The second chakra joins the yellow fire of our belly with the red of our life blood in a dance of creation. Ancient tantric literature describes this as the ecstatic union of the female shakti and male shiva, which gives form to the formless. Sex is representative of this union. Sex is ultimately creative. It brings new life. Orange stone spheres connect you with this creative, manifesting, bonding energy.

There really isn't a translucent orange stone that is good for gazing. Sometimes you can find an orange-colored amber or calcite, but seeing into it is difficult at best. It's best to visualize your clear sphere as orange. Orange stones make good charging spheres to be held or worn, and red aventurine, though it is called red, is perhaps your best orange color to use. It's plentiful and always very orange. Orange calcite has a nice color, but it's not practical. It's very soft and will scratch easily. Red aventurine is a hard stone. Orange-toned ambers don't scratch nearly as easily as calcite, but they are more expensive and usually not as true an orange as an aventurine.

Orange stones will help you visualize in your readings. If you charge your gazing sphere with orange it will help you be creative, because that is the natural expression of this energy center. Also, orange is a mixture of red and yellow, both strong fire colors, so orange-colored stone spheres are especially useful. If you find yourself getting tired during your reading, for example, hold your orange sphere and feel it feeding you energy. You can visualize soft orange light filling your body with warmth like a soft, sparkling fire. You see this fire entering the cells of your body so that they all look as if they're happily dancing. Feel as if this special aliveness fills every part of you. After a time of doing this meditation, just the feeling of the orange sphere in your hand or on your body will be enough to bring you to that state.

Wearing, holding, or gazing into a red-aventurine sphere will help stimulate your ability and impulse to bring new things to manifestation, whether they are ideas, artistic expression, or new projects. In my case, I feel that it is the creative impulse of my second energy center joined with the voice of my heart and the visions of my upper centers that compel me to write down the song I'm hearing or turn a vision into jewelry designs. Orange spheres can help stimulate that creative urge not only artistically but in business as well.

This creative energy is also one that helps provide the urge to bond with another in relationship. If your gazing is going to be focused on relationship in your reading, you might use heart-center spheres like rose quartz and green aventurine along with your orange sphere. If you're having trouble being in rapport with the person who asks you to do a reading, have them visualize with you an orange glow filling the crystal gazing sphere and then overflowing in all directions to fill you both in its light. Feel yourselves glowing with this orange light so much that it flows outward from you both in all directions, merging you together in an orb of orange light. Then the two of you together visualize the orange light changing to pink. Shift your focus back to the crystal ball and now visualize it glowing with the same pink light. Imagine bringing this rose-quartz-colored light from the sphere going into each of your respective hearts.

☺

RED JASPER, GARNET, AND RUBY:
LIFE-FORCE STONES

Red is the color associated with your first or "root" chakra or energy center that resides near the base of your spine. Roots bring energy to the tree in the form of nutrients and water from the soil. Roots bring life. In traditional kundalini yoga, it is this root chakra that contains dormant energy that must be awakened and activated to rise upward through each energy center until it rises from the crown to create a completely enlightened consciousness. The red fire can be seen as awakening the life force that lies dormant within us. Use it to charge dormant energies, whether they're physical abilities, unknown talents, or unearthed ideas, with new energy so that they come to life. If you reach a dull spot in your reading, use your red sphere as a charging stone and visualize sending life force into that area, breaking up the dullness.

In shamanic work these stones were sometimes referred to as "blood stones." Red was the color of healing, of life-giving blood, the blood that carries life force in the form of the oxygen that keeps us alive and washes away our impurities. It represents the blood that keeps us alive in the womb. As such, it represents safety and security and life itself. Use "blood stone" spheres like red jasper any time that you need to feel safer and more secure in life. I was taught a healing method, part of which involves being washed with red light, as if all your impurities were being washed away with the life-giving red blood of the Christ spirit. Charge your gazing sphere with red light using your garnet or red-jasper charging stone and gaze into it, feeling as if the red is charging you with the life force of the universe.

Red is also the color of fire. Ancient man used to revere fire as being precious. It supported life by giving both light and warmth. It was the hearth, one of your most basic supports and the center of your home. It represents life. But fire is not only life-giving, of course; it is also consuming. Fire destroys wood and anything in its path as it burns. If you want to use your crystal reading to break down, or "burn through" an issue or stuck place, use a red stone sphere or the red color in your gazing sphere to do it. Because of its color and its association with life force, stone healers have long used red stones for any work with the physical body that has to do with the circulation system, including the heart. Wearing a red stone or sphere like garnet, ruby, or red jasper, according to tradition, will help your circulation as well as charge you with energy. You can also use a red-stone sphere to charge up anyplace in your body that feels low energy or cool. Stone healers used to rub red spheres and stones over those areas of the body, warming up the cool areas and charging them with new life force. You can also do this with visualization and charging spheres.

Besides bringing life, roots also bring grounding. Many times when I'm gazing into my crystal ball and I start to feel as if I need some grounding and energizing, I'll hold a red jasper or garnet to balance me. Sometimes I'll even take a few moments to visualize roots going from the bottom of my spine deeper into the earth with each outbreath. With each inbreath I'll feel as if I'm filling myself with life-giving fire.

☻

BLACK AGATE AND BLACK ONYX:
SCRYING AND GROUNDING

I have spoken about black agate and black onyx many times throughout this chapter, but there are a few more things I might add. I have spoken of these spheres as being excellent for grounding, much more than the red stones. Smoky quartz has more of a gentle feeling as it grounds you, while black onyx and black agate feel more sudden, which can be a bit harsh or too grounding. To help gentle the effects of the black-stone spheres, you can combine them with a more heartful stone like rose quartz.

As I mentioned in the history section of this book, some gazers have used the black spheres for gazing. Instead of looking into them, you gaze off of their surface. Some scryers gaze using the light patterns reflecting off of its surface. Others feel as if they are being pulled far out into endless black space. Others feel as if they are gazing into infinity, the place beyond all beginnings and endings, where there are no boundaries or limitations. Once they enter into this place, the readings begin. Because these stones are the black of infinity, they are thought of as being able to lead you to other universes in your readings. In Native American symbology, black is the color of the west, the deep unconscious, that which is unknowable by the logical mind. Hold or wear your black-agate gazing, grounding, or charging sphere and visualize it opening you to those deeper levels of your consciousness, those areas that are normally inaccessible to your rational mind. Because you can use black-agate and black-onyx stones and spheres to go beyond the rational mind, you can also use them to stimulate your psychic abilities. Some gazers even wear small black-agate or onyx spheres on their ears, believing they will both ground them and help open their third eye.

This completes the list of color stones that are best used for spheres and some of the ways of using them. If you meditate with each sphere, you will continually learn more about it. The final thing to remember about colored-stone spheres is that they are useful tools, and like any tool, may make some things easier. However, as much as these colored-stone spheres can help you, you don't need to use them in your crystal ball gazing. All of the gazing that you want and the answers that you seek can be found in a clear sphere . . . and, ultimately, in yourself.

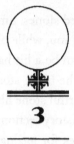

3

Choosing, Storing, and Charging Your Crystal Ball

When you choose a sphere for yourself, choose the one that simply appeals to you. Usually what attracts you is right for you. However, as I said before, it's good to know something about the different types of crystal balls so you can make a more educated decision. It makes your choice even better if you know how to harmonize yourself with the stones. Then you're choosing from a deeper place within you . . . which will make your relationship with your crystal ball that much stronger.

BEING IN HARMONY

As shamans and most indigenous people will tell you, every other life form in the world, stones included, "speaks" with us. This doesn't mean that they're talking in words. If a life form isn't physical, it's not going to have a physical voice. You're not likely to hear a normal human voice coming from your crystal ball, for example. But if you pay attention, if you bring yourself in some sort of harmony with any other life form, you can hear its "voice." There will be some sense of communion and communication. It may not be anything that you can verbalize but instead a certain kind of feeling, a sound, a sensation in your body or a picture in your mind. It's these kinds of impressions that we put words to.

An Andean shaman once taught me that it was important to take the time to listen to a stone talk to you. For hundreds of years his people, isolated from society high in the peaks of the Andes, had worked with their stones this way. He said that it wasn't unusual to see many of their shaman-teachers always walking about hunched over a stone held to their ear. He said that you'd even see them hold long conversations with their special rocks.

So, to listen to stones and crystals we stop talking. We quiet down by keeping our body grounded and centered, our thoughts and emotions quiet, and our awareness focused and open. This is especially true with crystal balls. In order to "read" them or "hear" them you have to be in harmony with them. It's just the same with people. Most of us are familiar with the feeling of being in tune with someone or not. If we're not in tune, the relationship just doesn't feel right. You often find in this case that you have difficulty understanding each other. It's exactly this way with crystal balls. Anytime before you do your reading you harmonize yourself with the crystal ball. In order to choose a crystal ball that will be good for you to work with, find the one with which you have the most harmony. Pay attention and you'll know.

☻

CHOOSING THE RIGHT BALL FOR YOU

My teachers taught me to be sensitive to the stones. They knew that I could have had all the instruction in the world, but if I wasn't sensitive to or in harmony with the stones I would never be able to work with them. This is true whether the stones were in totem form, raw or cut, crystals or crystal balls. Though each teacher had different ways of harmonizing with the stones, I noticed that the essence of each method was the same.

When you choose a new crystal ball for yourself, you can try one or more of these methods. Basically, to see if a crystal ball is right for you, start by holding it in both hands. Close your eyes and concentrate. Listen to your inner guiding sense. What sphere just intuitively feels right? What sphere do you seem to be drawn to? What crystal ball gives you a good feeling? I feel that the ball is welcoming me, almost as if it's giving me a big hug. If I'm holding it I don't want to put it down. I can't stop looking at it. This shows that you have a strong rapport with the sphere. This is not to say that you can't develop rapport or bring yourself into harmony with other crystal balls, because you can. I can read any crystal ball and so can most other practiced crystal ball gazers. However, generally speaking, your most powerful readings will come from the crystal ball with which you have the strongest rapport.

☺

CLEARING YOUR CRYSTAL BALL

As I explained earlier, your crystal ball will attract and store vibrationally within it any influence with which it comes in contact. These influences can be as varied as sound, light, touch, emotion, thought, or the surrounding physical environment. What influences your crystal ball will, in turn, affect you or anyone else who comes in contact with it. This can be both beneficial or harmful depending on the type of influence. If your crystal ball, for example, has been around a person who touches it and says how beautiful it is, it may transmit that feeling of wonder and appreciation to you later. Likewise, if it's held by someone harboring dark thoughts, you might start feeling depressed or angry during your next reading. These thoughts and feelings would affect the purity and accuracy of your reading. So, it's important before you do your reading to start with a "blank slate," a crystal ball that is free as possible from any other influences other than the focus of your reading. To this end you must "clear" your crystal ball when you first get it, before you begin to work with it and whenever it has been around any undesirable influence. Sometimes you may notice your crystal ball intuitively seems dull or to be lacking in vitality. Clear it then also.

Throughout my years of working with them, I have learned many ways to clear crystal balls. I find that the best method is smudging, which uses smoke from burning herbs or incense. Native Americans most often use the dried leaves of sage, cedar, or the dried grass called sweetgrass. Whether you use Native American herbs or others, choose the ones that make you feel uplifted, lighter, or in some way better when you smell their smoke. Smudging is a very simple method. First, light the herbs or incense on fire, then blow it out so that it creates smoke. (If you're using sage or cedar leaves, either put some of it on a piece of hot coal, or burn it in a heatproof bowl or abalone shell.) Then fan the smoke over your crystal ball, or move your sphere through the smoke, intending for it to become clear. At some point, usually almost immediately, your crystal ball will either look brighter or will just intuitively seem more clear. I usually smudge myself before and sometimes even after clearing my crystal ball. This way I clear myself of any feelings, thoughts, or other influences from the reading so they don't affect me later. When you are through, extinguish any remaining flame and smoke from your herbs or incense. Or, if you like, you can keep the smoke going, clearing your crystal ball or yourself as you go from one question to another in your reading.

☺

STORAGE AND HANDLING

Just as throughout history there have been many ways of clearing crystal balls, there have also been many ways to store and handle them, some very elaborate and ceremonial, others quite casual. In some traditions, crystal balls were considered to be moon-magnetic and were to be kept wrapped in black cloth. They never could have sunlight on them or be touched by anyone other than the one using the sphere. It was believed that if the sphere was touched or mishandled once that it was finished for good. The color of the cloth that you wrap your sphere in is important. Many traditions suggest that you wrap it in black. They believe that black is the color that will most effectively block any other vibration from influencing your ball. Others think of the color black as representing the unknown, the subconscious, deep space, or infinity. I wrap one of my gazing crystals in black. White, representing purity, is another good color to use. In some Native American traditions white is the color of healing, in others, red. I wrap my other crystal gazing sphere in white. Yellow represents enlightenment, so many feel it's appropriate to use this color. If you're not sure what effect a color has, meditate with it and see how it makes you feel. If that's a feeling that you want to have around your crystal ball, then use it. There are no hard-and-fast rules. If you don't know which color to use, use black.

My recommendation would be to begin by keeping your crystal ball covered when you're not using it. When you wrap your crystal ball or store it in a cloth pouch it's best to wrap it in natural fiber. Most prefer cotton, silk, or leather. You may want to store your crystal ball wrapped or unwrapped on an altar or in a special place that you've set up. That influence of purity and devotion will permeate it and carry into your work with it. It also gives some protection against intrusion. You may also want to include something with your crystal ball that has a special meaning or power for you. I keep a couple of my smaller spheres with other stones and a small statue of Quan Yin, the tranquil oriental goddess of compassion. Any crystal ball that you have set aside for a specific use shouldn't be touched by others and should definitely be wrapped. You wouldn't want to expose it to any other influences that might interfere with its special function.

After you have used your crystal ball for a while and grown

more sensitive to it, you can expose it to others, if you like, or even let them handle it. Just be sure to clear it before you use it and any time that it seems "clogged." It's perfectly all right to keep spheres out to energize a room or a particular environment. In fact, I recommend it. You may want to keep your charging spheres wrapped so when you use them you're getting the benefit of their color and other attributes without their being diluted by other influences. I tend to keep most of my gazing balls, when they're not wrapped, on a special altar where sunlight can get through them. I feel the sun is good for them, keeping them energized and charged with its pure golden light. I keep my eye on them, though. If I ever feel they are being clogged with something negative, I clear them with sage or cedar smoke, then again leave them to charge in the sunlight. How you store your crystal ball is up to you, because ultimately it's the strength of your focused intention that counts the most. It's stronger than any other influence. Listen to yourself and you'll know what to do.

☺

PROGRAMMING AND CHARGING YOUR SPHERE

You can deliberately put your crystal ball in contact with anything positive and it will be picked up and stored automatically to affect you positively later. Putting your crystal ball in moonlight, for example, charges it with those qualities associated with it, such as gentleness and intuition or all those things that you feel when you're under that light.

Some crystal ball readers, however, deliberately *send* something into their sphere to influence it a certain way to then affect them positively. This is called "programming" your crystal ball. When you're programming your sphere, you're consciously creating a new vibration or set of vibrations with your focused intention and sending them into the crystal ball. A crystal ball can be programmed with thought, emotion, sound, color, touch, other objects, or the elements. These can all be stored in the crystal ball for continuing effect. (If your sphere is glass you won't be able to program, charge, or energize it like this.) I gave you examples of such programming earlier when I spoke about charging spheres. If you want to send the color of the stone charging sphere into your gazing crystal ball, you visualize the color traveling into your gazing sphere as a stream of light. You use your willpower, or focused intent to send the stream of light. You can charge your sphere with an affirmation like, "I am clear, insightful, and perfectly focused," visualizing those feelings and thoughts entering the crystal ball. The stronger your focus, the stronger the programming. Your programming will be even stronger if you use your breath. If you're programming your sphere with a thought, for example, hold that thought in your mind, take a deep breath, and blow out gently. Imagine that your breath carries that thought into your sphere. Keep doing this until you intuitively feel as if it's enough, that the thought is well planted in your sphere. If you combine that thought with a corresponding feeling and then send that into the crystal ball too, your programming will be that much stronger. If you're thinking of love, for example, also feel it in your heart.

❤

ENERGIZING YOUR CRYSTAL BALL

To charge a crystal ball is to activate it or put power in it. Generally speaking, shamans don't feel that this needs to be done. They feel that the crystal ball is already a living thing, so it doesn't need any activating effort on their part. The crystal ball may need clearing or sometimes even "waking," but it's already alive. The shaman doesn't have to put power in the ball either. Like every other living being, it has power from its inception given to it by the Higher Spirit.

In my experience the crystal ball does have life force. It's not a dead object that you have to give power to. However, just like with a person, there are things that you can do to give it more energy, to awaken it as some shamans might say. Generally speaking, the same things that give you energy will give a crystal ball energy. I remember when I lived in an ashram it was our practice to get up every morning at three and jump into a cold shower before starting our meditations. As torturous as those first few moments were, when I got out of the shower I not only was completely awake, but I was full of energy. Even after a warm shower you feel refreshed and energized. You activate or charge your crystal ball in the same way by holding it under cool running water. Hold it in the ocean waves, in rushing rivers, under waterfalls, and even (in a pinch) under running tap water. Touching your crystal ball to the earth will not only help clear it, but will charge it with the nurturing energies of mother earth. Take your crystal ball and hold it up to the sun, letting its rays fill your sphere with light, charging it with solar power. Charge it with moonlight. Some shamans will even charge certain spheres with fire by passing them through a flame. This is especially appropriate for those spheres of yellow, orange, or red stones.

Though your quartz crystal ball will be charged to some degree just by being in contact with the water, sun, etc., the charging will be stronger to the degree to which you can consciously and one-pointedly focus on your intention that it happen. Concentrate on your crystal ball as you put it in a running stream, for example, intending that the water energize it. If you're having trouble maintaining your focus, you might say the words in your mind, "Energize, energize." A Native American medicine man might pray while he does it, "Spirit of the water, please give some of your energy to this stone so that it may be clear and strong." Likewise, if you're holding your crystal ball up to the sun, completely focus on the rays penetrating your sphere. When you're really focused, you can even feel it charging in your body. As your crystal ball charges or wakes up, you may begin to feel a buzzing sensation starting in your hands and continuing to move up your arms into your body. If this happens, plant your feet firmly on the earth and ground yourself.

☺

CHARGING A CRYSTAL BALL
WITH ANOTHER CRYSTAL

About thirteen years ago I met with another crystal worker who was trying, as I was, to bring crystal information out of the closet and into mainstream consciousness as much as was possible. We were quite good friends and liked to show each other our best crystals, exchange information, and generally play around with our stones together. He had a beautiful, optically clear natural-quartz sphere that I was admiring. Seeing that I was looking at it, he picked it off of the shelf and handed it to me. "See what you can read in here," he said, "and I'll show you something."

The sphere was so beautiful that I couldn't resist working with it, so I sat down across the room from him and, while holding it up to the light, began reading it. I first started seeing lots of images that didn't particularly have much meaning for me. So I kept looking for something else. I was pregnant at the time, so I decided that I would see if I could see my child-to-be. Soon enough I saw an image of a child with blond hair, blue eyes, and freckles across his nose. I promptly told my friend what I was seeing.

"Good! What else do you see about him?" He encouraged me to continue looking more. I kept seeing the same image, but when I tried to see more nothing came to me. This I told my friend.

"Keep looking and watch what happens when I do this!" he replied as he began unwrapping a clear-quartz crystal point. I kept my attention on the sphere, occasionally glancing at him to see what he was doing. I saw that he was pointing the tip of the crystal at the sphere I was reading from across the room where he was still seated.

"I'm charging your sphere with this crystal in my hand," he explained. I saw him intently focus on his crystal as he was saying this. "Continue reading now. You should be able to see more."

He was right! As soon as he started charging my sphere with his crystal I started seeing more about my child. I was able to see everything about him and was able to see him grow up through the years. (So far, everything has come true!)

This is an example of charging a crystal ball with another crystal. Occasionally I do it myself now . . . especially if I get stuck in a reading. I hold a quartz crystal in my right hand and point its tip directly into the center of the sphere. I focus on the crystal and visualize that it is sending energy into the sphere. If you are doing it right, you can actually feel a tension between the two stones, almost as though there is a connecting string between them. Sometimes, to help, I move the crystal in little circles, almost as though I'm spiraling the energy into the ball.

☺

CHARGING OR ENERGIZING
THE CRYSTAL BALL WITH YOUR HANDS

There are no rules as to when you should energize a sphere. Sometimes I energize my crystal ball before I start gazing into it, and other times I don't. I don't do it as a regular practice, but only if for some reason I feel my crystal ball needs it. It's an intuitive sense. The sphere just seems dull and somewhat lifeless, even after I've cleared it.

If that's the case, I put my hands on either side of the sphere and harmonize myself with it. I hold my hands firmly against the sphere and bring all of my focus into the crystal ball and my hands. When I feel that the contact is strong, I close my eyes and, with both feet on the ground, I visualize that the energy from the earth is flowing through my feet, up my legs, through my body, and into my hands.

Next, I imagine that the energy from the sky is flowing through the top of my head, down my body, and into my hands. I keep running both the sky and earth energies through my body until I feel them very strongly. (Sometimes when I do this my entire body starts vibrating with the force of it.) Then I open my eyes, focus my attention back into the sphere without losing the awareness of the earth and sky energies within me, and send that energy into the sphere. I sometimes take a deep breath and blow toward the sphere, feeling as if the energy is moving with my breath. I keep doing this until I sense that it's time to stop. This process doesn't have to take a long time, but it can be intense nonetheless.

Sometimes I find myself pressing the crystal ball fairly hard and it feels like both my hands and the crystal ball are buzzing. Sometimes I go into a light trance state just energizing the sphere because I'm so focused. When I'm through, I let go of the sphere and shake the energy out of my hands and clear myself again. When you charge a sphere this way, often you can see a difference. It looks brighter. Other times you can't see any change, but the crystal ball feels lighter and more charged.

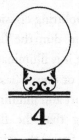

4

How to Read a Crystal Ball

PREPARING THE ENVIRONMENT

Before you sit down to do a crystal ball reading, take some time to prepare the environment around you. It's very important to make certain you won't be interrupted. Let the people around you know that you want to be left alone, that this is special time you are taking for yourself. Tell them you don't want to be interrupted unless it is an emergency—and be sure to let them know what you consider an emergency! Turn off the phone. Have someone look after the kids. Keep your pets out of the room.

The environment in which you'll be working should be peaceful and quiet, with nothing to distract you. I like to set the ball up on the table in front of me, in such a way that it won't roll. To stabilize the ball, use a stand designed for it, available from most stores that sell the balls themselves. Have absolutely nothing else on the table except perhaps a plain tablecloth. I often use a white cloth because I feel it doesn't influence the crystal ball with anything else other than healing or purity. The basic idea is that you don't want anything around that might distract your eye (and your mind) from the crystal ball.

Some people only do their readings in a silent room, such as one meant specifically for meditation and crystal ball gazing. The quiet energy of such a space can help you concentrate. If you like, play some soft, quiet, and uplifting classical or New Age music in the background. I prefer to dim the lights, then shine a light directly into the ball so that it is illuminated. You can use a candle behind the ball, a spotlight or even a flashlight. You can also purchase lightboxes that support and illuminate the ball. The ancient seers used candles, feeling that the flame provided a certain warmth, and the flickering fire of the wick, magnified by the ball, helped draw the reader into the ball's imagery. Though sometimes I enjoy a flickering flame, I think that the lightbox gives a most consistent and complete illumination.

Adjust the temperature in the room so that you are comfortable. You might note that sometimes your body temperature will drop slightly when you are in the meditative state of your reading, so you might want to set the room temperature slightly higher than you would normally prefer.

An alternative way of reading is to set up your room so the crystal ball is in or near a window, allowing sunlight to illuminate it. But a word of caution here: The crystal can act like a magnifying glass and can actually burn skin, wood, cloth, or other materials as the sun comes through it. It won't bother your eyes, because the sphere isn't lying directly against them.

If you have a limited time to do your reading, set a timer so you won't have to interrupt your focus constantly to check the clock. A good length of time for a reading is between ten and thirty minutes.

Have a small tape recorder nearby to record insights that come up for you during the reading. I highly recommend this because often you'll not remember all that you see. Even if you're doing a reading for another person who is present at the time, it's still a good idea to record that information so that the person can review it later. You'd be surprised how much we don't remember or don't even hear the first time around!

If you are doing the reading for another person, have him or her sit directly opposite you, with the crystal ball between you. Set the crystal ball about two feet away if it's a larger ball (more than 3" in diameter), and about one foot away if it's a smaller ball (1 ¼ to 3" diameter). Adjust the distance if you are near- or farsighted. You want to have the ball close enough to see into it comfortably, but not right in your face. I find that the ball is easiest to read if it is at chest level.

❂

DEDICATING YOURSELF

At the point when you have your physical environment set up, it is time to prepare yourself. Begin by asking the Higher Spirit for help and guidance. In a quietly inward way, ask that you may always be in the service of truth, honor, and wisdom. Ask that you not be led astray by your own desires or ego but be truly guided by the highest purpose. Some people do this in the form of a prayer. Others prefer simply to hold these intentions in their minds. I always like to charge my crystal ball with the following invocation or prayer. I feel that this sets the reading in the proper context, aligns me with truth and the Higher Spirit, helps me speak with discrimination, and charges the crystal ball. I recommend that you say this prayer or one like it before you begin any reading. As you speak this invocation aloud or silently, speak it from your heart, where it is most powerful. It is very powerful and grows more so every time that you say it. Here are the words:

INVOCATION

I dedicate this crystal ball to the service of my higher self.
I dedicate myself to the Higher Spirit.
I dedicate this reading to the higher good.
May nothing but goodness, insight and healing flow
*   from this reading and may no harm come from it.*
May the words that flow from my mouth be only those
*   reflecting Your wisdom and not my own desires.*
May the Truth be served.
Amen.

◉

PREPARING YOURSELF

Sit upright, with your spine straight, in a chair in front of your crystal ball. Rest your hands in your lap. Close your eyes and take two or three long, deep breaths through your nose. Gently and slowly exhale each time, relaxing your body more with every exhalation.

Relax your hands in your lap, letting all tension be released from your jaw, your face, your throat center, and your heart center. Relax the tension from each arm, down over your shoulders, to your elbows and wrists, then out through the middle of the hands and finally through the tips of your fingers. Breathe three more long, deep breaths, further relaxing your body on every outbreath ... your chest, stomach ... small of your back.

Let your hips relax. Feel the sense of relaxation going down your legs to your feet. With each outbreath feel all the tension leaving your body. Feel yourself growing deep, energetic roots, extending into the earth, flowing out from the tips of your fingers, the bottom of your spine, and the bottoms of your feet. These deep roots will keep you grounded and relaxed. This groundedness is essential for crystal ball reading.

Next, take three more long breaths, feeling the air move in and out of your nose, imagining your breath entering and leaving through the center of your chest, your heart center. Focus all of your attention on the middle of your chest, feeling as though all of your energy is being collected in the area of your heart to center you. Being centered is essential for your crystal ball reading.

Now shift your focus to the top of your head. Breathe in and out of the middle top of your head three times. As you breathe out, imagine that your head opens into a vast amphitheater of clear blue sky tinged with golden light. This will help open your higher intuitive energy centers. In this way you'll sit in balance, as if you were a tree, the roots deep into the ground, branches reaching high into the endless blue sky, your energy collected in your center, around your heart. This is the balance needed for your crystal ball reading.

At any time during your reading, if you become distracted by dizziness or shakiness, take a couple of breaths and send your roots deeper into the ground, from your feet, your fingertips, and the bottom of your spine. Then shift your focused breathing gently to your heart center to collect yourself. Once you are centered and grounded in these ways, you can turn your focus back to your reading. With practice, you'll be able to do it without losing your focus on the reading.

If you are doing the reading for another person, have them also breathe and focus in this way. You can guide them through this process as you do it yourself. That way you'll focus and calm their energy so it won't distract you from the reading. The best readings happen when the energies and intentions of both people are open, calm, and focused.

◉

HARMONIZING WITH YOUR CRYSTAL BALL

Once you are centered and balanced, take both hands, palm-to-palm, and rub them together very quickly for about thirty seconds. Your hands will feel like they're heated and tingly, warm from the friction of the rubbing. Focus your attention on your hands as you do this.

Now open your hands, palms up, and breathe very lightly over them, from your palms to your fingertips. This will sensitize your hands. When you are ready, place one hand on each side of your crystal ball. Feel the ball between your two palms, between your right and left set of fingertips. Move your hands a little away from the ball and see if you can feel almost a buoyancy and/or a slight breeze or buzzing sensation. When you feel that, set your hands lightly on the crystal ball on either side and, with your eyes closed, focus on the ball in your hands until you feel a gentle pulsation, as if the ball were lightly breathing in and out. At this point you have joined your energy field to that of the ball.

Now, begin rubbing the crystal ball with your hands, going round and round slowly, without letting go of your feeling of connection with the ball. Do this with your eyes closed at first, then open, looking at the ball. The ancient teachers used to say that this establishes an empathetic connection between the crystal ball and you. Not only are you getting to know your ball, but you are also implanting it with your vibration. Think of it as becoming friends with your ball, so that it begins to feel as if it's part of you. Once you have felt this, you are ready to begin your reading.

Another method used to harmonize yourself with the crystal ball is this: Sit or stand with your spine straight. Hold the ball in both hands, level with the center of your chest. Use the breathing method described above to center yourself in your heart, sending your "roots" deep into the earth and opening the top of your head to the sky.

Close your eyes. Imagine that your body has tendrils, or fine threads of energy or light. Imagine these threads of energy or light emanating from every surface of your body, extending in all directions as far as your inner eye can see. It's as if your body has no boundaries but is entirely made up of these energy strands.

Shift your inner focus, eyes still closed, to the crystal ball in your hands. Imagine that it, too, has these fine threads of energy or light extending from it deep into the earth, in every direction around it, and up into the sky. Visualize that the body of the crystal ball is also entirely made up of energy strands, just like your body.

Feel or visualize the unity of your energy body and the crystal ball's energy body, with your threads of energy interwoven. With your eyes still closed, allow yourself to feel it as well as visualize it. Open your eyes, still maintaining your sense of unity with the crystal ball.

If the crystal ball is small enough, you can also do the following to further harmonize yourself: After centering and grounding yourself, rest the crystal ball gently on top of your head. Breathe in and out, feeling as if your inbreath is entering through the crystal ball, then down into your head, extending even into your heart center.

Feel as if your outbreath is leaving your heart center, up through your throat, then out the top of your head, extending through the crystal ball and out into space. Again, feel a sense of unity between you and the crystal ball. This practice will also tend to balance and open your heart, making it more compassionate and empathic, increasing your intuition and psychic abilities while expanding your consciousness into other realms of reality.

If your crystal ball isn't too large or heavy, there's another way to harmonize with it. It begins with centering and grounding yourself, then gently and slowly rubbing the ball over the entire surface of your body. The shamans of old said that your eyes are not the only organ of seeing . . . so is your skin. As you rub the crystal ball over your body, allow your skin to "see" the ball. Feel it against your body, noticing any impressions, visions, or feelings that come to you in the process. Don't worry if they make sense or not, just notice. You will not only get information about your ball, you will soon feel as if you are intimately acquainted. Again, it's as if the ball becomes part of you.

Some ancient traditions say that each crystal ball contains its own spirit. They also say that every being in the universe, seen and unseen, has its spirit. This is true of people, animals, plants, and stones. If you get in touch with the spirit of the crystal it will speak with you and tell you all about the ball. This spirit has no form and isn't an entity, but it does have a definite reality. The shamans of old would contact the spirit of the crystal ball, attuning themselves to it by using one of the methods above. Then they would hold the ball over their heart center, over the top of their head, or against their ear, asking to hear from the spirit, and listening with their inner sense of knowing, until the spirit of the crystal ball spoke to them through their hearts. In this way the spirit of the ball would assist them in their reading. Much as with people, they warned, if you were not respectful of the spirit voice, not working from a place of love and harmony with the divine will, the spirit would turn on you and cause you harm. That warning holds true not only in working with the spirit of the crystal ball, but with all forms of crystal readings. As the saying goes, what you put into the crystal ball, or what frame of mind you work with, comes back to you at least tenfold.

THE TRIANGLE OF ENERGY

Once you have harmonized yourself with your crystal ball, place it back on the table and focus the light on it. As you do this, move slowly, maintaining your focus on the connection between you and the ball. Now you are ready for the last step before you begin the actual reading of the crystal ball.

Take two or three breaths in and out from your heart center. Imagine that your heart is connected to the place in the ball that you are gazing into. Next, imagine that the center of your forehead, also called your third eye, is connected to that same place in the ball. Take a few moments to feel the triangle of energy between the center of your forehead, your heart center, and the crystal ball. This way of linking yourself with the ball will help you keep focused on your inner sense of truth, and will help you to be aligned with your psychic and intuitive insight. It is from here that you will receive your deepest wisdom in your work with the crystal ball.

All this may sound tremendously time-consuming. But you will find that the process quickly becomes automatic, moving smoothly from one step to the next. It may take you twenty or thirty minutes at first, but with practice you'll quickly get it down to four or five.

Each sitting will be easier and faster than the one before. Have patience and don't worry. You may also find that when you're tired it's harder to maintain your focus. So, at least in the beginning, try to choose times when your energy is high. After all is said and done, you'll find that with repetition and tenacity, you will be doing it as easily as you get dressed in the morning. Besides, even the first time you read the crystal ball, you'll enjoy some interesting results.

☺

BEGINNING TO DO A READING

Now you are ready to begin the actual reading. Briefly close your eyes and, placing each hand on either side of the crystal ball, feel its slight pulsation. Then rest your hands in your lap.

Open your eyes, still maintaining your inner focus, and look inside the crystal ball. Find an area that interests you. If you wish, you can slowly move the crystal ball around until you find an interesting area. When you've found something that interests you, or for some reason you just want to stop—perhaps for no reason at all—stop moving the ball and look into that area. Focus your eyes in the area that interests you and look at it more closely. What do you see?

If you want to lean closer to the crystal ball, do so, but keep your spine straight. However, don't lean so closely that your eyes cross and don't get any closer than six inches from the ball. If you do that, instead of seeing more, you'll see less.

As you continue looking into the ball you'll find that your vision begins to grow more and more diffused. At this point you may not see details in the same way. You may have impressions; you may see symbols that will recall things to you. Instead of figuring out what the symbols mean, just look further into the crystal ball, recording your experience.

At this point you may begin to feel as if there is no longer a separation between you and the crystal ball. It may feel as if you're inside it, or inside a clear sphere of light with no edges or boundaries. You're just there. When you are inside the crystal ball like this, you are in a trance state, very present in the moment, with all your attention pouring into the ball, unaware of anything else around you.

As you read a crystal ball, you may feel a tugging in the center of your forehead, almost as if you're being gathered there, as if someone were pulling a thread out of a piece of cloth, causing a puckering. Some people feel as if the center of their forehead is spiraling outward. If this begins to bother you, relax your jaw and your neck, your chest, and the small of your back. Feel the roots of energy extending out of your feet so that you're grounded again.

Relax your ears, the back of your neck, and even the top of your head. Use your breath to facilitate this, imagining that you are sending your healing breath to those areas of tension. After grounding yourself, breathe two or three times out of the center of your forehead, until it feels as if your head is opening and filling with clear blue sky. As you crystal gaze more often this sensation will pass. Just as when you start a new physical exercise that challenges a weak muscle, these parts of your body will also strengthen in time.

There are many ways to describe what it's like to be "inside" a crystal ball. It is sometimes compared to being in a beautiful sky, with clouds of different forms and shapes. A crystal ball will have a thousand times more than the cloud, though. It seems incredibly vast once you get inside, as vast as the universe. To me it's like stepping into a limitless space. It's very clear and filled with light. When I feel that way, I like to feel that I'm opening my heart and filling myself with pure peace.

☙

WAYS OF SEEING

There are also many ways to see into a crystal ball. In fact, the word "see" is misleading. Rather, what we perceive is more like having strong visual and nonvisual impressions, or seeing pictures in your mind's eye, even if those pictures seem to originate in the crystal ball. You may even hear sounds or have a sense of sounds. You may experience temperature changes.

Another way of seeing is to use the crystal ball as your doorway to an inner seeing, continuing to use the crystal energy to keep you focused. Here is this method: First, fix your focus in the crystal ball until your vision diffuses or grows indistinct. Then close your eyes (or they'll close naturally), and envision the crystal ball in your mind's eye, sitting in front of you on the table, just as it was when last you viewed it. Visualize that crystal ball getting larger and larger, until all you see before you is the ball. It continues to grow larger until all you see is a wall of crystal in front of you. There are no edges, it's so big. Then, as you look, imagine a door opening in front of you. In your mind's eye, walk through this doorway and close it behind you.

Now you are in a total crystal environment. Look around and notice that parts of the crystal look like landscapes or other objects, or even clouds up in the sky. Visualize a crystal chair before you, and sit down in it. Then begin to breathe as we talked about before, establishing your roots in the crystal ground, opening your heart center, then your crown (top of your head) into the vast crystal sky.

While bringing your attention to your heart, let yourself go into this infinite crystal space. You may feel like you're floating or flying. Or you may feel as if you're sitting comfortably at home in your chair, or on some other surface. You may find yourself in other worlds—that is, in worlds that seem unfamiliar to you.

Don't try to analyze what's happening at this point. Let yourself be, just as when you're outside, sitting in your chair at home, reading your crystal ball. Let yourself just be inside this world. Begin to record your impressions or what you're seeing and experiencing. Begin to ask your questions. If you are having trouble getting an answer for your questions, picture that a large crystal book opens in front of you, and turn the pages until you find your answer.

Another way to read a crystal ball is to work with the veils and inclusions in the crystal ball. Once you have attuned and aligned yourself with the crystal ball, look at the details formed by these inclusions or veils. Once you find something that interests you, look at it in more detail. Look and see where it leads you. Once you're in the trance state, these details will begin to suggest things to you—faces, landscapes, outer space, or situations that answer your questions. If you see a landscape, find a pathway that you can follow inward as you look more closely. Follow this pathway through your landscape deeper and deeper into the ball until your vision diffuses and what you're seeing grows less distinct and you're seeing mainly with your mind's eye. Your eyes may or may not close.

It really doesn't matter which of the above methods you use. Over time, you will probably develop a style of your own. I have at one time or another used all of these methods. Now, when I start my reading, I don't even know ahead of time what method I'm going to use. I just start the process and see what happens. I try not to have expectations one way or another. That way I don't limit my experience. In spite of the fact that I design jewelry and am a strong visualizer, when I am crystal ball reading I tend not to see pictures in the ball. Instead I get strong impressions of sound or sight. I like to use the veils and inclusions as pathways inward, but most of the time I soon find my eyes closed or my vision so diffused that I'm seeing entirely with my mind's eye.

One of the most valuable lessons I've learned—and one that I have to learn over and over again—is that there is no right or wrong way to see. What matters most is that you enter the trance state. This is important because you need to free your mind from linear thinking so that you can access other ways of knowing.

ASKING QUESTIONS

Once you are in the crystal ball, you can start asking questions or focusing on the reason that you are doing the reading. Bear in mind that you don't always need to have a question in mind to do a reading. Sometimes I just use the crystal ball to relax, to free my mind or open up my creativity. (Other practical uses for crystal ball readings are discussed later.)

When you are asking questions or looking for solutions to a problem, know that the answers you get from a crystal ball are there inside you all the time. They may seem to come from the crystal ball, but the ball is actually just a tool. It is helping you get in touch with a level of awareness or consciousness that we usually cover up in the busy-ness of daily living.

When you link your mind with your heart, and go beyond linear thinking, you move into the present; you start living more in the moment, in the here and now. In that way, you are able to go past the constrictions of the mind, past what you believe your world to be, and past all limitations and expectancies. It's like taking a leap beyond.

When we go beyond the linear mind, we're able to know things beyond what can be known by more linear ways of perceiving. Likewise, if someone else is asking the question and you're using the crystal ball to answer it, know that you are just helping them access the answer that is already inside them. However, the crystal ball helps you to focus in a way, to be in a particular way that allows these answers to emerge.

It is peculiar to the human mind that most of what we create—including our problems!—come out of what we have stored in our minds within very particular patterns of thought and feeling. When we can't find an adequate solution to a problem we're facing, or we want something more exciting than what we already know, we need to go outside those patterns of thought and feeling. But it is very difficult to do that. We've come to depend on the old patterns, and our mind keeps pulling us back to them. It is only by tricking our minds with devices such as the crystal ball that we can momentarily step outside these patterns. We literally empty our minds and create a space for new forms to enter. It has also been suggested that by our going into this not-knowing state, our old patterns are shuffled around like a deck of cards, providing us with a brand-new game.

Crystal ball gazing is a tool that helps you open up, allowing you to perceive nonstructured realities, that is, material often referred to as the "invisible reality." It is a little like gazing through a window into the intuitive realm, the world associated with feelings, intentions, dreams, and spirit. The experience of crystal gazing includes all possibilities of seeing, hearing, and otherwise sensing things differently than you ordinarily would. It is a way to go beyond what your rational mind says is possible and thus move into the intuitive, creative, and mystical realms, depending on how you wish to use it.

The moment you relinquish your linear way of perceiving the world and go through the doorway that takes you into a reality beyond the rational mind, everyday understanding falls away. You begin to experience a world that you cannot know in the traditional sense. Indeed, you may not be able to describe the parameters or give any particular shape or form to this other world.

People sometimes ask, where does the new information come from that fills the empty space we create through crystal ball gazing and other intuitive tools? There are many ways to answer this question but the bottom line is that the answers are always there. The universe itself holds them at all times, just as it holds the mysteries of life and death. Our patterns and habits of thought prevent us from receiving all but a tiny portion of those answers. That's why going into a state of not-knowing is so important; it allows us to stop clinging to that limited portion of knowledge we've come to depend on and open our hearts and minds to another little piece, perhaps, that the universe itself holds.

Another way to understand crystal ball reading is that you are using it as a tool for accessing your subconscious or intuitive knowledge. Many consciousness researchers have noted that the human brain is a kind of filter; without it we'd be receiving all the knowledge of the universe all the time. With so much information flowing in we wouldn't be able to function at all. However, when we go into the crystal ball to that place of not-knowing, we in effect bypass the filter and allow new information to fill us. We have only to enter the world of the subconscious or intuitive to receive it. (Again, this subject will be explored in more detail in the succeeding chapters.)

So when you ask the crystal ball a question, do so with the knowledge that you're asking yourself a question, or you're asking the universe a question, or you're asking higher intelligence a question. The answers are always there; it just requires this special kind of openness that the crystal ball provides.

A large part of successful interpretation is asking your questions properly. Not only is it important to ask your questions without adding your own emotions, but it's important to ask as directly, simply, and clearly as possible because the answer that you get will directly reflect all of the parts of the question that you ask. If you don't frame your questions so they are direct and simple there will be so many complications that your question may be unanswerable with any clarity or accuracy. You may really have asked several questions in one and there may even be parts to it or implications of which you're completely unaware. A simple question may call up other events or elements that you were unaware of, but you can track them down and make sense of them. If you do have a complicated question, ask it in one step at a time.

When words, images, or sensations start flowing back to you in answer to the questions you've asked, and you begin to describe what you're getting, try not to let your mind revert back to the rational and linear. Don't stop the flow by trying to interpret or "understand" what you're receiving. Just record your observations.

You must allow total freedom for whatever is coming through to come through. Think of the information as a river and you want to allow yourself to be carried along in the current. Swim with the current, not against it. Analyzing it will create a dam that diverts the flow. When you're swimming, just swim.

Sometimes you find that as you gaze into the crystal ball, the original question you asked suddenly ceases to be very important, or the answer comes almost before you can verbalize it. Many times in questioning, it's all done nonverbally because the answers are there as soon as you can frame the question. You may find yourself responding, "Yes . . . ah-hah! Oh yes, this does make sense!" Often you'll find yourself with questions leading to other questions or subquestions. And you hear just "yes" or "no," or you get a sense, "No, go that way," or, "Go this way."

Sometimes the responses you receive are nonverbal impressions that only later become verbal. In fact, you don't always understand how the impressions even relate to the question you've asked. If this happens, just record your impressions and later meditate on them to come up with your answer. Of course, in the process of verbalizing a nonverbal impression you've received, you are forced to use the linear tools of your mind, upon which language is based. At this point, interpretation becomes an issue. Any time we interpret an image, the chances are pretty good that we're putting our own "spin" on the information, which may very well be a distortion. The question then becomes, how do we polish our lens so that we are minimizing distortion? The answer is that we at least get closer to clarity and truth through practice and through reexamining the information we receive.

Pure information from a crystal ball reading doesn't have to come right at the time of your reading. You may only get a piece or part of it. You may only see a part of your vision. So record your vision or your impressions and then later meditate with it. See what it tells you. Sit with it, contemplate it, let yourself dream about it, so that it continues to reveal newer and newer understandings. Each time you review your information you may understand more of its meaning.

Once you believe you understand the messages you've received from a reading, you don't necessarily want to stop there. Keep a record of your initial impressions. Go back to the original "data" again and again because sometimes you can reach new understandings even years later. It's much like going on a meditation retreat or a vision quest. What you get from it doesn't always come in the moment. It can take hours, weeks, or even years for you to fully grasp the experience.

It is important that you don't use crystal ball reading in place of your own common sense. I've explained it this way many times: Just because you've decided to believe gravity isn't real (based on your reading), doesn't mean that you'll suddenly start floating! If you know you're allergic to dairy products, for example, and you see in the crystal ball that you should be drinking lots of milk, common sense would tell you that you're probably wrong. At the very least, test your information. In this case, you might try taking a few sips of milk and see if, in fact, your allergies won't erupt. Also you might want to try doing another reading to see if you get the same information.

If all this sounds a bit complicated, let me assure you that with just a little practice the whole process becomes far easier to do than to explain.

☺

THE MIND'S EYE

While you are doing a reading, your "seeing" is a mixture of messages from the Higher Spirit as filtered through the screen of our own ways of experiencing, understanding, and explaining the world. In other words, our inner vision is a mixture of pure input and our own screening. This is what is called our "mind's eye." Because of the functioning of your mind's eye (we've all got one), when you are reading a crystal ball, as much as you are receiving information, you are also adding information.

When we crystal ball gaze, we do three things: (1) view pictures, receive impressions, or otherwise perceive information, (2) distinguish our own projections, desires, expectancies apart from other information so we can perceive more clearly, and (3) interpret the information. Since the information in our readings will always be shaped by our own mind's eye, doing an accurate reading can be tricky. You need to trust what you see unquestioningly during your reading, even as you know that what you see is being formed to some extent by your own projections, desires, and expectancies. You might see in your crystal ball, for example, a ship that suggests to you that you are going to take a world tour. However, the ship might really mean that your life is going to go through a major transition, and you only saw a world tour because that has been a lifetime dream of yours. The tour was your projection. This process of filtering with desires and expectancies can both help and hurt and makes it even more important to test all your information afterward in the "real world" before taking anything as the truth. Even if you're free-associating, which is a form of projection, you're doing so knowingly in order to unlock your intuitive mind. Eventually, as your intuitive mind becomes more active, images and ideas will seem to flow toward you instead of from you. Pay attention to them, sorting imagination, free association, and other personal input from true content. As long as you are aware of and are willing to let go of your own projections, you'll be able to improve the "purity" of your readings.

How to do this? Practice, practice, and more practice . . . and patience. There are also a couple of other things that you can watch for. If you find yourself asking a question over and over in order to get a "better" answer than the one that was given to you, it is usually a sign that you are desiring a particular answer. This desire will get in the way of your reading because when you get the "better" answer, all you are really receiving is the amplification of your desire, not the truth. If you find that you are asking your questions with any emotions that you may be feeling, you can be sure that your answer will merely be an amplification of your own emotion. For example, if you ask your question in frustrated terms like, "Why doesn't this person love me?" you'll receive the frustration you feel and the frustration of the question amplified in a frustrated answer . . . all at once! Your reading, then, is nothing more than a reflection of your frustrated state of mind. Instead, ask your questions in a nonemotional manner. If you find yourself trapped in some emotion that you can't clear, stop your reading until that emotion passes. When you do read with this type of dispassion, you have the feeling that the impressions come into your inner eye and then flow right out of your mouth without any interruption . . . a river of information that keeps flowing through you as long as you stay "tuned in."

☙

INTERPRETATION AND SYMBOLOGY

When you crystal ball gaze, you are using the ball as a focusing device to center yourself, calm your mind, concentrate, and "see" from a larger perspective than your normal consciousness allows. This, however, is only one part of the process. As you might have gathered from the previous chapters, the interpretation of what you see is just as important, if not more so, than the initial "seeing" of the information. Some people see pictures in the crystal ball that are accurate depictions that can be taken at their face value. For instance, if you look into your crystal ball and see your lost wallet in your top drawer, it's pretty clear. Go look in your top drawer to find your lost wallet. Strong impressions that you receive are very often this straightforward as well.

More often than not for most people, however, all or part of their reading comes in the form of symbology. If you ask your crystal ball, for example, what you can do to facilitate a better communication with someone and you see a rabbit, it doesn't mean that you should go get them a rabbit. It might mean that you should approach this person more gently and that they are rather timid. The rabbit, in this case, makes sense only symbolically.

The way to work with symbology is to let loose your logical mind and free-associate. In this case, ask yourself what a rabbit means to you. Let any associated thought or feeling come forth without censoring it. What qualities does a rabbit have? Imagine that you're a rabbit and see what you feel like. What does it remind you of? What other associations do you have with a rabbit? As you continue to do this, you might find lots of information just from the one rabbit that will teach you about your communication with this person.

If we have the proper perspective, everything can become a symbol for us that we can use in our readings and in our daily life. When you start to work symbolically, you'll start noticing what's around you in an entirely new light! If you change your perspective you can learn from this experience. Study the coincidences in your life, for they can be doorways to the unknown.

Even though any symbol can have endless meanings and meanings unique to the one perceiving it, it can sometimes be useful to study what others understand symbolically. I have included a chart of many common symbols that have been used in every form of scrying and divination, not only crystal ball gazing. I include this chart not because these meanings are etched in stone, but so they may stimulate your psychic flow. When you see one of these symbols in your reading, you can refer to the chart to see what they might mean. If the particular symbolic translation has meaning to you, use it. Or you can use these meanings as stepping-stones to arrive at your own. Enjoy!

SYMBOLS AND THEIR MEANINGS

Acorn	Happiness, health, wealth
Airplane	A journey without risk (if broken = with risk)
Alligator	Treachery
Anchor	Stability, security, peace of mind
Angel	A guide, spiritual help, blessings to come
Ant	Reward for hard work, cooperation, perseverance
Apple	Success, prosperity, moral decision
Arrow	Bad news, a message
Ax	Danger, trouble ahead
Baby	A new project, a beginning, addition to the family
Bag	Acquisition, confinement, a trap
Ball	Varying fortunes, indecision
Barn	Material goods, safety
Basket	(Full) A gift is coming, abundance
	(Half full) Short-lived worries, temporary setback
	(Empty) Money worries, lack of abundance
Bat	Danger, warning
Bear	Retirement, hibernation, love, mothering
Bed	Laziness, time to rest, hiding from life
Bee	Busy, cooperation, success with friends or groups
Bell	Announcement, news arriving, marriage
Bicycle	Forward movement, proceed cautiously
Bird	Freedom, good news, peace
	(Caged) Entrapment, frustration, confinement
Boat	Refuge, travel, help in difficulty
Book	Information, education, discovery
Boot	Protection, dismissal, leave-taking
Bottle	Fascination, illness, good "medicine" coming
Box	Confinement, a gift, possession, uncertainty
Branch	An addition, a veering away from

Bread	Contentment, good health, nourishment
Bridge	Understanding, joining, a new start, success
Broom	Clearing away, disappearing worries, beginnings
Building	Security, a new living or working arrangement
Bull	Stubbornness, quarrels ahead, a stubborn problem
Butterfly	Transformation, innocence, pleasure, beauty
Cage	Entrapment, a proposition, stuck energy
Cake	Celebration ahead
Camel	Perseverance, slow to understand, news arriving
Candle	Showing the way, illumination
	(Broken) Losing your way
Car	Travel, transition, change in surroundings
Cascade of Water	Intense emotions, disappointed efforts
Casket	Death, transformation, bad news, failure
Castle	Wish fulfilled, only a fantasy, rising to authority
Cat	Intuition, false friends, an ambush, relaxation
Cemetery	Death, transition, an ending
Chain	Events connected, a joining, marriage, a prisoner
Chair	Being held, time to take it easy, a guest
Chicken	Ability
Child	A new beginning, innovative idea, innocence
Chimney	Prosperity, "going up in smoke"
Church	Spirituality, understanding, faith
Circle	(Unbroken) Completion, continuous happiness
	(Broken) Betrayal, disappointment, leave-taking
Climbing	(Uphill) Good luck, progress
	(Downhill) Bad luck, failure
Clock	Avoid delay, death, recovery, hurry, illness
Clouds	Illusion, doubt, problems, not clear-seeing
	(If heavy or dark) Misfortune
Clover	Luck
Clown	Simple pleasures, happy, pretense, not serious
Coin	Abundance, prosperity, success, money

Column	Success, arrogance, support, ethical concerns
Comet	Unexpected and sudden happenings, speediness
Compass	Travel, new direction
Cooking	Watching your health (especially digestive)
Corn	Successful harvest, prosperity and abundance
Cow	Equanimity, increased abundance
Crab	A warning, pain, interference in love
Cradle	A wish coming true, taking care, children
Cross	Sacrifice, trouble ahead (usually emotional)
Crow	Trouble on the way, falsity, forewarning
Crown	Success, authority, that which rules
Crying	Happiness or unhappiness, relief
Cup	A new friend, holding, finding fault, happiness
	(Full) Success
	(Empty) Shortage
Curtain	Obscured vision, not seeing the whole picture
Dagger	Betrayal, danger, impetuousness
Daisy	Love ahead, hope, simplicity
Dancing	Light spirit, plans turning out well, enjoyment
Death	Long life, transition
Deer	Gentleness, shyness, beautiful soul
Desk	Work or business projects, study needed
Devil	Evil, frustrations lasting awhile, unhappiness
Diamond	Purity, wealth, insight
Dice	A gamble, a loss
Dish	Nourishment, an invitation
Diving	Going forward in spite of risks
Doctor	Good or bad health
Dog	Faithful friend, loyalty
Doll	Looking for a mate, time for fun, phoniness
Donkey	Patience, foolishness
Dove	Peace, forgiveness, messenger of love
Dragon	Self-deception, challenge, prosperity, beginnings

Drum	Quarrels in the air, time for a change
Duck	Persistence, "staying afloat," a fortunate sign
	(Pecking duck) A warning, persistence needed
Dusting	Making it clear, revealing, a revelation
Eagle	A spiritual sign, realization, freedom, insight
Ear	Someone talking about you, listen!, hearing
Earth	(Standing on) Nurturing, grounding, abundance
	(Seeing from space) Perspective, peace, let go
Egg	Fertility, prosperity, good things to come
	(Broken) Failure, birth, manifestation
Elephant	Gentle strength, loyalty, anything with memory
Evil	(An appearance of) Warning, remember to love
	(Feeling of) Fast change needed, remember to love
Explosion	A blowup is coming, metamorphosis, big impact
Eye(s)	Wisdom, psychic intuition, seeing, Higher Spirit
Eyeglasses	Need to see more, understanding needed
Face	A guide, helper or friend, introspection, illusion
Fairy	Joy, light spirit, romance, playfulness
Falling	Something not working, changes, letting go
Father	The Creator, protection, provider, male energy
Feather	Showing the way, good fortune, air or sky quality
Fence	Boundaries, holding in, limitations
Finger(s)	Pointing the way, a warning, indicator(s)
Fire	Great energy, heat, rapid change, life force, anger
Fish	Fluidity, yielding, Christ spirit, love
Flag	Warning, keep your integrity, a signal
Flies	Annoyances, lack of attention
Flowers	Love, delicacy, tokens of affection, soothing
Flying	Being free, letting go, ecstasy, going fast
Foot	Keeping up, walk on, stop what you're doing
Fox	Cleverness, untrustworthy, humorous
Frog	Jumping to conclusions, quick moving, good luck

Fruit	Plenty, materialization, nourishing
Garden	Incredible bounty, happy heart, success, joy
Gate	Beginning of a journey, arriving home, a test
Gems	Good fortune, clarity, wisdom, wealth
Goat	Stubbornness, moving forward, unstoppableness
Gorilla	Strength, good humor, bluster, threatening
Gun	An attack coming, the end
Halo	Angelic presence
Hand	Help is on its way, a friend, healing energy
Harp	Angelic influence, romance, sign of heaven
Hawk	Hunting, keen vision, warrior, danger threatens
Heart	Love, compassion, fulfillment, passion, the heart
Hill	Obstacles ahead, effort is needed
	(On top of) Perspective, success, vision
Horse	A true friend, a lover, a male friend
	(Dark horse) Disappointment, bad luck, longshot
Horseshoe	Good luck
House	Shelter, success, family
Human figures	Take your cue from their appearance, activities and surrounding environment and symbols
Ice	Clarity, cold, brittle, a cold exterior
Insects	Pesky problems, warnings, earth spirits
Jail	Confinement, getting caught, a bad conscience
Jars	Containers (take your cues from what's inside)
Key	Discovery, the way through, fortune, a new home
King	The ruler, a controlling person or influence, male
Knife	Cutting through, betrayal, separation
Ladder	A climb, a promotion, a way up
Letter	A message (read it for cues), sending or receiving
Lightning	Inspiration, high energy
Lion	Ruler, strong will, family, the hunter
Lizard	Earth spirit messenger, patience, a mistake
Lock	A secret, something closed, security, obstacles

Man	Creativity, male energy (see "human figures")
Mask	Something is being hidden
Mermaid	Water goddess, flirtation, beauty, temptation
Mirror	Looking at what's in front of you, illusion
Monkey	Mischief, fun, silliness, lightheartedness
Moon	Intuition, romance, feminine energy, rest easy
Mountain	Major obstacles, highest vision
Mouse	Timidity, petty theft, gentleness
Music	Listen—how it makes you feel is your message
Nest	A place for rest and security, home building
Net	Gathering, be careful of traps
Numbers	Take your cues from other symbols
Owl	Wisdom, loss, intuition, "night vision"
Ox	Strong will with gentleness, a hard worker
Palace	Serenity, material success, protection
Parrot	Gossip, scandal, brilliance
Peacock	Luxury, vanity, beauty
Pig	Mixed luck, greed, selfishness
Pillow	Rest needed, peace, luxury, sleep-related
Purse	Money, spending
Pyramid	Mystical initiation, success with solid base
Queen	Ruler, controlling person or influence, female
Rabbit	Gentleness, love, fun-loving friend, innocence
Rainbow	Astral and spiritual vision (go into it, take cues)
Ram	Leadership, going forward, majesty
Rat	Treachery, warning sign, deviousness
Raven	Messenger of the Spirit, warning, mystery
Ring	A wedding, completeness, change for the better
Road	A path to take
Rock	Steadiness, immovability, fear, firm, problem
Rose	Love, romance, beauty, a good sign
Rowboat	Be patient, it will take time but you'll make it
Scales	Balance needed, weighing the options (take cues)

Scissors	Quarrels, failure, cutting apart
Sheep	Docile, following without question
Ship	Travel, "staying afloat"
Shoe	The body, having to do with walking
Snake	Spiritual energy, knowledge, treachery, distrust
Spider	"Dream weaver," guile, persistence, wealth
Square	Balance, protection, peace, look in all directions
Star	Joy, prosperity, inspiration, recognition, heaven
Storm	Difficulties but calm ahead, disturbance
Sun	Creative energy, the power of God, health, heat
Swan	Longtime partnership, romance, love, contented
Sword	Fighting, anxiety, a warning, "cutting away"
Table	Company, eating, a meeting, communion
Teapot	Good friends, discussions, take it easy
Tears	Disappointment, hurt, happiness, loneliness
Throat	Communication, speech
Throne	God, authority, "hot seat"
Tiger	Fierceness, inner strength, danger, hunting
Toad	Flattery, hangers-on, ugly
Tortoise	Slowness, don't take shortcuts, thoroughness
Tree	Good health, strength, related with all life (take more cues from type of tree)
Triangle	(Point up) Success, balance, excitement, reward
	(Point down) Missed opportunities, bad luck
	(look for signs inside of it for message)
Trunk	A journey, fateful decision, subconscious
	(Something inside for you to find)
UFO (or flying saucer etc.)	
	Other worlds, space
	(look for cues to see what your message is)
Umbrella	Protection, a shield
Veil	Something hidden, illusion, unconscious, sad
Vine	Success, intertwinement, strength, fruitful

Vise	Strangling emotions, closely held
Volcano	Something's about to blow up, potential anger
Wall	Go no further, a blockage, interruption
Watch	Time orientation, stay watchful (look at the time for other cues)
Water	Referring to the emotions, "washing away," travel
Web	Intrigue, something caught, interconnection
Whale	Ancient memory, wisdom, "record keeper"
Wheel	Karma, cause and effect, travel, inheritance
Wind	A message, spirit, clearing, breath and lungs
Window	A new view, an opportunity, escape, intuition
Wings	Angels, "flying away," escape, message, spirit
Wolf	Greed, hunger, savagery, hunting, nobility
Woman	Intuition, female energy, mother (get cues from her and surroundings)
Worms	Guilty conscience, dissipation, imbalance, illness

☺

YOU'RE NOT GOD

When you are doing your reading and interpreting it's important to remember that you aren't God. You are trying as much as you can to be accurate, but you are fallible. You may be wrong or mistaken in what you're seeing. Your interpretation may be completely wrong. You may be reading your own projections instead of really tuning in to the other. In order to avoid playing God, remember to offer yourself and act as if you are just an empty conduit for the Higher Spirit. You are merely reporting your impressions as they come to you, while weeding out any personal agenda or projections. This is a very important point, because it is a trap that is easy to fall into.

It is also easy to fall into the trap of exaggerated self-importance, especially if you're insecure or feel unloved or unnoticed in your life. Doing the reading for someone, especially if you seem to have answers or abilities that they don't, can make you feel important and special in a way that you don't feel in the rest of your life. Your ego gets fed. When you're caught in this trap it can be very obvious or it can be as subtle as false humility. Be aware of this and try to catch it and put a stop to it. Try using affirmations or prayer and get some extra help for yourself.

EXITING THE CRYSTAL BALL

Generally speaking, back out of the crystal ball in the same way that you entered. For example, if you entered the crystal ball by envisioning it getting larger and larger until you were inside it, you can continue that vision until you're through gathering your information. See the crystal around you, then a crystal wall in front of you, then visualize an opening doorway. Some people feel as if they're floating in the sky when this doorway appears before them. Either way, pass over the threshold of this door into the world outside. As you go out through the doorway, see the crystal wall behind you, which becomes a large crystal ball. See the crystal ball shrinking smaller and smaller until it is exactly like the actual ball that sits on the table in front of you.

Recall the room in which you are sitting, then recall the chair or other surface on which you are sitting. Feel your feet on the floor and feel as if you have roots into the earth. Bring your attention to your heart center. Now take two or three nice, strong breaths, inhaling and exhaling through your mouth. Then open your eyes.

If you went into the crystal following a pathway suggested by the veils and occlusions, visualize finding the same pathway and backing out of the ball, following that path. Let your vision stay diffused, and continue to back out. Follow the path out until you become aware of the edges of the ball. Then bring your focus back to your heart center and then back to the chair or the surface on which you are sitting. If you're leaning forward, straighten up and bring your vision gently away from the ball. Let your vision be clear rather than diffused. Before you leap up, just sit quietly for a moment. Get yourself centered and grounded in the same way that you started.

If you are using a clear ball with no veils or inclusions, use your intention alone to back out until you're aware of the ball's edges, then the entire ball. Clear your vision and bring your focus back to the room you're sitting in and to the chair or other surface you're sitting on. Center and ground yourself.

In all of these methods the important thing is just to sit a few minutes with your full consciousness in the room around you and with full body awareness. As you breathe normally, eyes open, you might want to gently flex and relax the muscles in your arms, your hands, your legs, your stomach, and so on, until you feel normal physical sensations returning. It is important to get yourself grounded again. Don't dash right out and drive your car, cook on a stove, or anything where you might encounter a physical hazard.

Take a few moments to thank the Higher Spirit for the help and vision that you received. Then pray that you (and the other person, if that is the case) are able to use wisely the information you gathered and do so in the service of the highest good.

☉

A FINAL WORD

As you can see, the crystal ball can become much more than just something used for fortune-telling or divination. It can become a very useful tool to get beyond our notions of how things should be that our rational, linear minds seem to demand. We can use the crystal ball to travel far beyond the mind and the restrictions it creates within us and within our world. We are able to use the crystal ball to go from a world of structure and limitation to a world that is unstructured and limitless . . . where everything is possible. The more we consult the crystal ball in this way, the more our capacity to receive these new forms of information is enhanced. We're freed to experience our lives more deeply and to expand ourselves beyond what we had ever imagined. We're freed to use our minds more powerfully and completely as we unify the rational with the intuitive. It's like having a life without the walls that restrict us. If nothing else, crystal ball reading is endlessly fascinating, allowing us to become acquainted with that world of imagination and dream that is the birthplace of all creativity.

5

Practical Applications—Everyday Uses for Crystal Ball Gazing

Although a crystal ball is thought of in mystical or psychic terms, it is also a tool that can benefit you in your everyday life. You don't have to be connecting with spirit guides, astral traveling, or foretelling the future. Here are some of the ways that you can use your crystal ball that are very down-to-earth. Try them out and see what you experience. And these aren't the only ones. Once you have tried them out you'll understand the general principles and be able to find practical uses that are specific to your own life.

CALMING YOUR MIND AND THINKING MORE CLEARLY

This is one of the easiest things to do with your crystal ball. It is also one of the most important, because it can have far-reaching effects on your health and peace of mind, something hard to find in the pressures of daily living. Often our mind goes into overload and thoughts start whirling around so rapidly that we can't stop them. We have no clarity at all, only confusion. To be able to think more clearly, we have to be able to slow down our thoughts and calm our mind.

When you gaze into a crystal ball, your mind "slows down" as your concentration increases. Because of this effect, gazing into a crystal ball can be specifically used as a meditation practice to bring your mind to a state of absolute calm, clarity, and acceptance. Using your crystal ball this way is similar to an ancient form of meditation called Vipassana or "mindfulness." In Vipassana meditation, you sit quietly with your spine straight and drop all focus on anything else other than the flow of your own breath. In this crystal ball meditation you sit likewise, quietly dropping all focus on anything other than what you see in your crystal ball. Unlike other crystal ball work, here you do nothing other than gaze. If you see visions, you just observe, letting them appear and disappear. Likewise, if you hear things, or feel things, as soon as you notice them, drop your attention from them and bring it back into the ball. As in Vipassana meditation, don't try to figure anything out, or "do" anything. Just keep gazing into your crystal ball.

Some people carry around a smaller, hand-sized crystal ball for just this purpose. Anytime their mind needs calming they pull out the sphere and gaze into it until their mind becomes still and peaceful. I know one woman who holds a lot of responsibility in a very busy office. She wears a crystal ball pendant, and whenever she has so much on her mind that she can't think clearly, she holds the ball in her hand and uses it to clear her mind. Sometimes, she takes a few moments to gaze into the ball, but most of the time she finds it easier and less conspicuous just to hold it. Once her mind slows down, she feels her thoughts are more ordered and she can more clearly see the answer to a problem or make a difficult decision. She's been so amazed at the difference this makes that she always tells people, "Never make a decision with a crowded mind!"

CHANGING YOUR STATE OF MIND

Using your crystal ball to change your state of mind is done the same way as using it to calm your mind. As an artist owning a business, in the course of a day at the office I usually have to switch back and forth quickly from my creative mind to my more analytical business mind many times. I might be in the workshop with my jewelers, creating a new design, for example, and I get a phone call or have to attend a meeting that requires financial or management decisions. When that happens, I go into my office, and before I pick up that phone or attend that meeting, I ground myself, then gaze into the crystal ball that I keep there. As I gaze, getting more and more concentrated into the ball, I empty my mind of every thought about what I was designing. Sometimes, to help empty my mind, as each thought comes to my attention I take a breath and blow it out slowly, letting the thought go as I do it. This helps clear my mind even more. Once my mind is clear and calm, while still gazing into the crystal ball, I shift my attention to the new direction. I recall the problem that needs solving, for example, or the financial data that I have to consider. Continuing to gaze into the crystal ball, I let go of all competing thoughts about designing as they come to my attention, and shift them back to the problem or financial data. Once I feel that I am sufficiently focused in the new direction, I stop my gazing and attend the meeting or begin that phone conversation. Once I'm through with the conversation or meeting, I repeat this crystal ball gazing process to shift my focus completely back to the designing.

Now, this sounds as if it would take a long time to do. Sometimes it does, but usually it doesn't take long at all, especially if you are a practiced gazer.

☻

STEPPING OUT OF AN EMOTIONAL WHIRLWIND

Crystal ball gazing is a good thing to do when you don't know your own feelings or when you have too many feelings. Maybe you're feeling hurt and can't seem to recover, or you're so angry that you can't think straight or so numb that you can't feel anything. Crystal ball gazing can help you to reach buried feelings, help you to understand them and transform them.

Many times we block our true feelings because they're too intense, or we feel bad for having them, or we're afraid to reveal ourselves. Sometimes they hurt too much, or we felt abused, hurt, or victimized and are defending our heart. It helps to remember this: Even though feelings may seem more real than anything else because of their intensity, they are no more permanent than your passing thoughts. They come and they go, flowing through us like passing clouds in a sky. Feelings have a tremendous effect on our health, thinking, sense of well-being, relationships, perceptions, and actions. So we need to pay attention to them, but remember how they change. Emotions are as valid a method of feedback as our logical mind. They are a guiding force in our life, so don't dismiss them. Just understand them.

In order to work with your feelings you have to know what they are. If you're not clear about them, stop thinking with your head and start feeling with your heart. You can do this with your crystal ball if you focus on both your third eye and your heart center, the center of compassion, empathy, and love, which will begin opening. If you've blocked yourself from your feelings, you'll start feeling them again.

To work with your crystal ball to help you feel what you've blocked, gazé into it until you feel concentrated. Without dropping your focus in the sphere, relax the small of your back and the area in the middle of your chest. Still focusing in the crystal ball, let your heart open. Sometimes it helps to feel yourself relaxing and opening on every outbreath. Feel as if there is a strong connection between your heart and your crystal ball. Some people visualize a beam of·pink light from the crystal ball to their heart. Others just feel it.

At this point, if you want to discover what your true feelings are about a particular situation or person, with your focus still in the crystal ball and your heart open, imagine that person or situation inside the crystal ball. Use your mind's eye. Or just have a sense of them while focusing in the ball. Now, pay attention to how you feel. Describe to yourself everything about how you feel, even if it doesn't make sense or if you don't approve of it. If that feeling had a voice, what would it be? Keep opening your heart and let everything come out. If you're concentrated, it shouldn't take you more than a few minutes to be clear about how you feel.

Sometimes we can get stuck in one emotion or another and can't seem to get out of it. Anger and anxiety are feelings that a lot of people are dealing with these days. You can get so anxious, for example, that everything that happens to you triggers your anxiety. Pretty soon you can't get out of it. It's a self-perpetuating cycle. Your anxiety makes you anxious. Your anger makes you more angry. Whatever the emotion, you're trapped in it. It's grown so large that there seems to be nothing else.

If you find yourself stuck like this, just gaze into your crystal ball, letting your emotions go in the same way that you let thoughts go to calm your mind. Take a few deep breaths and let them out slowly, releasing any emotion or thoughts and any tension in your body as you slowly breathe out. Then shift your focus to your heart center. This process will calm down your emotions enough so that you get centered again in your true self and see beyond your emotions. You'll get enough distance from them and be enough in the present moment that you experience a larger perspective again.

Sometimes our immediate feelings are so strong that we fail to notice any of the more subtle underlying feelings. It is these feelings, the ones that we often don't consciously know we have, that can drive the more conscious feelings. In order to work with the more overt feelings, then, we have to unearth these underlying feelings and bring them clearly to our immediate consciousness.

Gaze into the crystal ball to quiet yourself, then, maintaining your focus, call up the troublesome emotion or emotional pattern and see what underlies it. Do you have any feelings other than the most obvious? If these feelings have a voice, what would it say about itself? What are they trying to tell you? Look into your crystal ball and ask to see any life experiences that may be connected to these emotions. The more you learn, the more these emotions will lessen their hold on you.

☻

RELAXING

Once you've relaxed your mind and emotions, it's a natural thing for your body to relax also. So just the process of centering, grounding, and calming your mind and emotions that you do in crystal ball gazing brings the body into a state of alert relaxation.

Sometimes, though, in crystal ball gazing the opposite happens. Even though your mind and feelings are quiet, the more you gaze, the more you tense up. Sometimes you're too tired and you don't have the energy to do a reading. I've had this happen myself, often if I do readings when I'm tired. Other times, just handling the daily events of life are causing the tension.

No matter the reason, there is a good way to use your crystal ball to relax your body and fill it with a sense of well-being. I usually put both hands on my crystal ball and imagine a soft, golden light entering through the top of my head, moving slowly down through each part of my body until my entire body is filled. As this light fills my body from top to bottom, I lower my hands to my sides, and visualize it sweeping out everything that's negative or dark, replacing it with light. Still gazing into the crystal ball to maintain my concentration, I scan my body, and relax any place that feels stuck, as if it is holding on to something. I don't try to analyze anything, I just let go. If I have trouble letting go, I imagine that a golden beam of light comes from my crystal ball into that tense place, dispersing and disintegrating the tension. (If I'm really focused, sometimes I get "flashes" of insight and vision that tell me why that area is stuck. I analyze these later, though, rather than stopping the relaxation process.)

There are a few areas of the body in which some amount of tension is usually held. So when I systematically relax from head to foot, I never leave out these areas. This is what I do: Gazing into the crystal ball, I visualize golden light entering through the top of my head, slowly sweeping down through my body, clearing and relaxing all my tension as it does. This light fills my head, then my forehead and eyes, jaw and neck, my shoulders and the insides of my elbows, causing all the tension and darkness to drain from my fingertips into the earth. This light flows down my spine, relaxing the middle of my chest, relaxing my stomach and the small of my back, sending all the tension or darkness to drain down into the earth from the bottom of my spine. Keeping my gaze strong into the crystal ball the entire time to help me stay focused, the last thing I do is let the golden light sweep down my legs as I relax my pelvis, the back of my knees, and my ankles. Then I let all the rest of the tension and darkness drain from my feet deep into the earth.

Once I sweep the golden light all the way down through my body I like to continue gazing, and as I look into the ball I feel myself begin to radiate with this golden light so it not only fills me but extends out around me. Sometimes I put my hands on the crystal ball again, letting its energy help charge me with this light. If I stay focused, I start feeling very light, almost as if I'm floating. I feel totally relaxed and peaceful. Of course, the trick is to keep this feeling with me afterward!

One crystal gazer I know carries a smaller crystal ball in her pocket and anytime she feels herself tensing up, she puts her hand in her pocket around her crystal ball, takes a few breaths, and relaxes her body. She feels, as she holds the crystal ball, that it's helping fill her with light, and that it helps her focus. She says that she does it at her office and no one even notices, probably because it only takes a few moments and she can do it right there at her desk. She told me that it's like taking a minivacation!

If you choose to carry a crystal ball in your pocket, don't worry about how you're supposed to hold it. There's no particular way. I carry crystal balls and other stones around in my pockets from time to time and I find that usually when I hold them, I end up squeezing and turning them around and around in my hand. It just seems to happen automatically.

☺

ENHANCING CREATIVITY

Creativity is like an unending river of energy that you can tap into for never-ending insight and vision. This is an energy that is already in existence, not something that we make happen in some way. Many scriptures describe it as akin to the life force of the universe, always present around us, but only available for our use if we can be conscious of it. There isn't one kind of creative energy for writing, another for music, another for design, etc. It's all the same energy. You just form or express it differently depending on your particular talents. The point is to open up to the energy.

I use my crystal ball a lot to help me be more creative. Just by gazing you stimulate your third eye, the subtle energy center associated with, among other things, intuition and creativity. This will help open you to the creative flow. I know lots of people who don't consider themselves gazers, but still keep a crystal ball near them when they do anything creative, looking into it in order to free their mind. I regularly keep a crystal ball next to me when I write. I feel the crystal gives me energy. Even more than that, however, whenever I get stuck I just stop where I am and gaze into the crystal ball. As I gaze, I free my mind of everything I was saying and thinking and let it rest empty and clear. This is just the same process that you use when you use the crystal ball to change your state of mind.

After I've rested my mind for a few moments, I focus on my topic afresh, while still gazing into my crystal ball. Soon all these new ideas start coming to me. Sometimes I "see" them. Other times, something inside of the crystal ball, perhaps a veil or inclusion, will suggest things to me. In any event, I don't try to analyze the impression right away. I just let the visions and insights keep flowing until a new idea, a new story line, or a new way of saying something is completely formed.

FINDING LOST OBJECTS

In our house I'm the official finder of lost things. All I do is gaze in the crystal ball and track them down. I look into the crystal ball, letting go of all my other thoughts and feelings and start narrowing my focus down to whatever's lost. Sometimes I imagine it inside the crystal ball and then try to see what's around it. Other times, I'll start by asking for help, or I just think about the lost object. Either way, as I gaze, I start getting impressions of where it is. Then, I ask questions that help me narrow my focus more and more until I know exactly where it is. In the case of a set of lost keys, for example, I could tell that they were enclosed in something. I asked my husband if he had checked his desk drawer. He had, so I looked further into the crystal ball and got a strong intuition of their being in his closet. I told him to go look and then I suddenly "saw" him walking in the door wearing his blue pants. Then I knew where the keys were. "Check your blue pants. I think your keys are in the pocket." Sure enough, they were.

FINDING LOST PEOPLE

Using crystal balls to find people has a long past and an active present. The techniques used today to "see" a lost person in your crystal ball are the same that the fortune-tellers used to track down thieves, stolen goods, and missing people during the Middle Ages. They are the same used by the ancient shamans. Even today crystal ball gazers and other psychics are asked to help search for lost people or crime victims. Plenty of modern police departments still use crystal ball gazers and other seers for this reason.

To do this, you use the crystal ball the same way that you do to find lost objects. Focus in the crystal ball, clearing your mind of anything but the person as you search for them in your crystal ball. As with finding lost objects, pay attention to every impression that you get in any form, and don't analyze your thoughts. Just report your visions, feelings, and impressions. Analyze later.

OPENING YOUR HEART TO LOVE

Sometimes it's scary to love. We're afraid of getting hurt, or already have been hurt. Sometimes we feel too vulnerable and we're just not ready to let down our guard. Sometimes we want to love, but we're too angry or judgmental. Sometimes we feel numb, or as if we don't know how to love. Some of us have even made a conscious or unconscious decision not to love.

When I was growing up, I remember feeling there was no such thing as love that would last. I closed my heart against the hurt, but inside I felt such a longing! That longing is what got me into my spiritual search. I was looking for a love that would always be there, one that I could depend on. When I learned to open my heart, I found waiting there just what I was looking for . . . a love that would never leave.

I also saw that I had been going about it backward! Instead of waiting for someone to bring me love so I could open my heart, the job was *first* to open my heart and *then* to bring that love to the relationship! Instead of joining with someone as two incomplete people trying to be whole, you join as two people already whole. It's a joining *in* love rather than a joining to *find* love. When you're joining in love you're coming from love. When you're trying to find love you will never find enough.

There are many effective ways to use your crystal ball to help you open your heart to love, to fill the empty hole and bring a sense of wholeness, no matter how large your fears. These ways open you to the love for yourself, the love of another, and a love that never disappears. (It's all the same love!) One way is this: Gaze into your crystal ball and, when you're focused, feel as if a stream of light flows from the ball into your heart center. As you continue to sit, feel as if this light is softening and opening your heart, filling it with peace. As you do this, relax the middle of your chest and soften your belly. Let go of any other thoughts or feelings that pull you away from this love and light filling your heart.

This can be a very powerful experience, depending on your degree of concentration and your ability to let go. I remember one woman calling me up to tell me that after she had done a crystal ball meditation in one of my workshops, she had finally uncovered the feelings that had been bottled up for over a year since her father had died. I know that when my heart first opened I couldn't stop crying and laughing, because I felt so good. As your heart opens, many times feelings that have been held back come pouring out. If this happens, don't worry, your heart won't break. It's stronger than you think. Let these feelings come out, but don't dwell on them or get lost in them. After they come, let them go. Don't push them away or deny them, just let them go in their own time and keep bringing your focus back to the crystal ball.

If you're with someone and you both want to open your hearts more to each other, you can sit on either side of your crystal ball, and while gazing in it, each one of you use the light to open your heart, filling it with love. As you begin this connecting process, fears, resentments, old arguments, defensiveness, justifications that come between you may arise. As you let go of these and other thoughts, you'll feel yourself softening and opening toward the other. Go ahead and let yourself feel vulnerable. Once you feel as if your heart is open, continue to gaze and feel the beam of light connecting your heart with the crystal ball, and through the ball to your partner's heart. Feel as if your two hearts are joined together in this beam of light, each filled with the same light. Sometimes it's tempting to talk, especially if you are getting new understandings about your relationships or about love. But don't say anything right away. You may cut short your experience. Just sit there with each other, your hearts joined in love.

I have done this quite a few times. It's a wonderful way to connect very deeply with another person. I usually find that I eventually start breathing in sync with the other person. Sometimes the crystal ball seems to start pulsating, as if it's breathing right along with us. Sometimes you feel an amazingly strong sense of unity, within yourself, with the other person, and with everything and everyone else. You feel you could hug the entire world.

☙

IMPROVING COMMUNICATION

My husband and I are starting to do this when we find ourselves at odds with each other. Of course, you don't have to do this only with your mate, but with anyone with whom you are in a relationship. When my husband and I do this crystal ball process we sit at our kitchen table with the crystal ball on the tabletop between us. Sometimes we join hands and other times we just set our hands on the sphere for a few moments, then put them in our laps. We stop arguing or discussing our problem(s). Instead, we both silently gaze into the crystal ball, letting our minds and feelings be still and our hearts open. Sometimes it's hard to open your heart, especially if you feel hurt, mistrustful, defensive, or angry. When you can let go of your thoughts and feelings as you continue to focus into the ball, you'll start feeling more peaceful, and then it's easier. We find that it's good to be patient and don't try to rush the process. Then, with our concentration still focused, we try to put ourself in the place of the other person. There's an old Indian saying, "Never judge a man until you have walked a mile in his moccasins."

As we each gaze into the crystal ball, we begin to feel a sense of unity instead of separation. We see that we're not deliberately trying to hurt each other, we're just two people doing the best that we can. Every time that this happens we realize we're on the same side again! It's like starting afresh.

Then, while still gazing in the ball, after a few minutes of silence to let our understanding grow, usually we find ourselves rewording what we were trying to say, understanding how the other person can best hear. We're able to move out of our old, ineffective communication loop and into a place where we're truly trying to understand and be understood. When we crystal ball gaze together this way, we feel joined together again and without any need to build barriers.

☺

HEARING THE TRUE MESSAGE

There is a very important principle about communication: You have to *want* to be understood in order to be understood. Sometimes, for example, you can say things that are meant to hold people away, or that are meant to hurt; even with words that sound good on the surface. You can withdraw yourself, refusing or afraid to communicate, using silence as your way of speaking, or you can keep talking so much that the other person can't get a word in edgewise. Words like this are not a bridge, but a barrier. They are not designed to create an understanding, but are designed either consciously or unconsciously to keep you away in one fashion or another. The real communication lies underneath the words.

Sometimes when I encounter this roadblock I try not to react right away, especially if I'm confused. Instead, I later gaze into the crystal ball until I'm sufficiently focused to see myself and the other person in the crystal ball reenacting the situation. As I review it, I let go of emotional reactions and defenses. I don't repress them, I just notice them, then let them pass. I see what understandings come to me. I pay attention to any impressions or feelings in my body that come to me. If I'm really focused in the crystal ball, I start understanding other things about the communication that weren't apparent at first.

☙

DEVELOPING ONE-POINTED CONCENTRATION

I've already talked about one-pointed concentration, and I don't want to belabor this topic except to say that just in the process of gazing into your crystal ball you'll develop the ability to concentrate very quickly and completely. After all, concentration usually falters because other thoughts, senses, or emotions intrude, or sights or sounds distract you. When you look into your crystal ball and let everything pass from your attention except what you see in the ball, you are increasing your ability to concentrate. The more you can concentrate in the crystal ball, the more you can concentrate everywhere in your life. The benefits are enormous. When you can concentrate one-pointedly, decision making and problem solving become easier and you are less easily distracted. Your mental processes become more effortless; your logic is sharp and thinking is easy. Your mind becomes clear and strong. It may take some time, but it does happen.

❂

SENDING AND RECEIVING MESSAGES

Once you are practiced with your crystal ball, it is a fairly simple matter to send and receive messages. Back in my early twenties I had a friend who used to practice this with me. We set aside a month and chose a time every night when we would take turns sending and receiving. The first night I sent a message to him. I gazed into my crystal ball until I was completely focused in a trance state. Then I thought of a simple message and, still concentrated, I "thought" it into the sphere with clear, focused unwavering intention, and then intended that the message go directly to his crystal ball and into his mind's eye. I didn't only think about the message in words, but also visualized it as well. I also used my feelings, so that the words, visualization, and feelings would all reinforce each other and would more easily result in a total reception of my message (which was that I wanted to go sailing in the bay in my friend's blue sailboat). In other words, instead of just thinking about a blue sailboat on the bay, I pictured it in my mind and felt what I would feel when sailing, and then sent my mind's picture and my feelings into the ball as well. The more completely I could focus, the stronger my intention and the stronger the sending.

At the same time, my friend would gaze into his crystal ball until his mind was perfectly clear and wait for any impressions or visions that seemed to be a message from me. Sometimes he would seem to hear the message as an inner voice; other times he'd see things in the ball. At other times he would just have a strong impression. We'd do this for a half hour, and then call each other to see if he did, in fact, receive the message that I was sending. We would reverse the process each day; one day I would send the message and the next day he would.

At first we weren't very good at it. We wouldn't get the right message at all, or we'd just get part of it. (In the case of the sailboat, all he received was the color blue and a happy feeling.) After time, though, our accuracy improved so much that we'd get at least some part of the message right every day. The more we practiced, the more we could concentrate enough to send clearly, and the more we developed the inner "ears" and "eyes" to hear and see. After a while, we could pick up most of what the other person was sending, although sometimes interpretation became a problem. We'd receive the mental picture the other was sending, for example, but attribute another meaning to it.

You can use any kind of quartz crystal ball to send and receive messages, although it's easier with a more powerful ball. Some crystal balls contain phantoms (pyramids) and other inner shapes that will help you send messages. You can visualize yourself entering the crystal ball and then the pyramid. When you can see yourself inside of the pyramid, look upward toward its point and send your message out from there. It makes a very powerful launching pad. I remember one sphere that I worked with had an inner inclusion that looked like a rocket ship. I used to visualize sending my message into the rocket ship and then having it take off to deliver my message.

When you're sending a message, even if the other person isn't aware of receiving it, it's possible that it's still received on some level. I remember one time I started feeling a little uneasy, but I couldn't explain why. Later I found out that another crystal gazing friend of mine had actually been trying to send me a warning message that I didn't hear. Instead I picked up the feeling content in the form of unease. You don't have to be trying to send a message in order for it to be sent either. If you're focused in your crystal ball and you happen to think of someone, sometimes the thought goes right out to that person because the crystal ball gazing has so empowered it.

◉

SENDING POSITIVE AFFIRMATIONS OR PRAYERS

Many times, when I know a person is troubled I send prayers or positive affirmations through my crystal ball. I gaze into the crystal ball, think of or visualize that person, and then, while seeing them in the ball, pray for them and imagine that my prayer surrounds and fills them. When I'm sending an affirmation, I see them receiving it in my crystal ball and then I see them acting as if the affirmation has already taken effect. Sometimes I don't know what affirmation to use. When that happens, I visualize the person inside my crystal ball, see if I can tune into their feelings, and then let the affirmation come to me. If I'm patient, the affirmation always comes to my mind. If you don't know what to say, just send love. That, in itself, is a prayer.

You can also create an altar or sacred space where you place the other person's picture. You can write the prayer or affirmation on a piece of paper and place it over or under their picture. Then hold a smaller crystal ball in your hands, send the prayer or affirmation into it and place it over both the picture and the piece of paper. I like to light a candle and put it next to the crystal ball, paper, and picture. You can place other small crystals around the picture, pointing toward the crystal ball, further charging it with your prayer or affirmation. You can leave this up for any length of time that you think necessary. Every day, or any time that you feel you need to, you can use smudging to clear the crystals and crystal ball of any influence other than the prayer or affirmation that you chose. Traditionally, when you are through you should clear your crystals again and burn the paper with the affirmation or prayer on it, sending it to the Higher Spirit.

A good way to work with prayers and affirmations for yourself is to wear a crystal ball pendant over your heart center that has been programmed or "charged" with whatever prayer or affirmation that you want to affect you. To do this, first clear your crystal ball pendant, then hold it and gaze into it. As you do that, say your prayer or affirmation aloud, sending it into your sphere, where it will be stored. Then, as you wear the pendant, feel as if those prayers and affirmations go right into your mind, body, and soul. Each time that you feel it against your heart center, or see the pendant, or hold it in your hand for a few moments, you'll be reminded of your prayers or affirmations. If you like, each time that you are reminded, say them to yourself aloud or silently and keep sending them into your pendant. Doing this, you can keep the prayers and affirmations going constantly all through your day. Some people feel as if the crystal ball pendant not only serves as a reminder and stores the prayers and affirmations, but amplifies them as well, making their effect upon you even stronger.

PROSPERITY—OVERCOMING SURVIVAL ANXIETY

Survival anxiety is important to talk about here because it is one of the foremost recurring problems faced by people in what is often felt to be a competitive society.

Prosperity has less to do with the amount of money that you have than with your state of mind. If you don't already feel prosperous, no amount of money, possessions, or any such wealth will bring you that feeling. Prosperity is an inner sense of security and abundance that can only come from a strong sense of inner worth . . . which is the natural result of being in contact with your inner self. The opposite of prosperity is survival anxiety, which ultimately can only happen when you're out of touch with your inner self. Most of these crystal ball methods help you, even when it's not their main point, to feel prosperous because, ultimately, most of them are about your inner self and a related higher consciousness. When you relax, for example, your heart can open. When your heart is open you can reach your Self. So to be prosperous, the first step is to feel prosperous. When you feel prosperous, you begin to attract abundance to your life in all its forms and to feel that life is filled with riches of all kinds.

Doing this crystal ball meditation will help bring you prosperity and a sense of inner abundance. Gaze into your crystal ball until you are clear, calm, and focused. Gaze deeper and deeper until you feel as if you're inside of it, crystal surrounding you on all sides. Now, while you are inside the crystal ball, maintaining your meditative state, visualize a lush, kelly green light, like the light of mother earth appearing to swirl around you, then flowing through your heart center, filling your body. Floating in an ocean of green, feel your heart open and flood with feelings of self-forgiveness, great worthiness, joy, and abundance. See golden coins dropping, featherlike, about you, and open to the abundance of the entire universe. Sit for a while, basking in this feeling, soaking it into you so you'll be able to carry it with you after the meditation is over. When you are ready to end the meditation, bring all of the green light into your body and leave the crystal ball.

☺

HEALING

There is so much to say about healing and crystal balls that an entire book could be devoted to the subject. I have touched on healing earlier in the chapter about the types of crystal balls, giving you some information about placing crystal balls on the body, about using color and energy balance. My crystal book, *The Complete Crystal Guidebook,* covers much more. There are lots and lots of methods to work with healing. Central to them all is the idea that every illness (disease) is a result of imbalance or disharmony. When the body, mind, heart, and soul are brought back into a state of harmony and balance, healing will occur. Healing isn't something to be forced, it happens automatically when the conditions are right.

When you do your crystal ball gazing, with its emphasis on centering, grounding, calming, and clearing, you are bringing your body, mind, heart, and soul back into balance. So some amount of healing will naturally happen. However, you can work specifically on healing with your crystal ball. You can use it both for diagnosing and doing the actual healing work.

Gaze into the crystal ball until you are focused, calm, open, and centered. From this balanced state, continue focusing into the crystal ball and prayerfully ask that healing come to whatever part of you needs healing. Then, continue to sit in that prayerful, concentrated state and open yourself to receive the healing in whatever form it takes.

Healing will come to you; however, it may not take the form that you expect. That's why when asking for healing, it's important to feel yourself as healed, but not limit that process by envisioning exactly how it should take place. You may think that you need to heal your sore throat, for example, but the true problem may be the unshed tears you are carrying. The true healing, then, would be to heal your heart and, in the process, your throat will clear up.

I've done crystal healing work with people for years, and invariably this is the kind of thing I've experienced. I use the crystals (and crystal balls) to help bring in the healing energy and reestablish an energetic balance in the body. At the same time that I do this, I use the crystals to help diagnose the real problem. I open my mind past its ideas of what obviously needs healing so I can see what really needs working on.

You can do this yourself. Gaze into your crystal ball, centering and calming yourself, then meditate with it, letting all your thoughts come and go until your mind is clear. Then ask your crystal ball to show you the problem. The answer may come in many forms. You might see actual or symbolic visions, or just have a strong sense. As with all crystal ball reading, don't immediately try to make sense of what you experience. Just note it and analyze it later.

Often I find in my crystal ball work that what needs work isn't the body at all, but something else in your life that is out of balance. That's the root problem that ultimately needs correcting. I remember working with a woman who had been diagnosed with a cervical precancerous condition. I worked with my crystals and crystal balls, but what I saw was that something in her life was sexually out of balance. When she cleared up the sexual problem as well as doing the stone work, her cervical condition cleared up. Another woman I remember had very bad arthritis and migraine headaches. Besides working with the stones, I saw her in a very bad relationship that was causing her a lot of pain. When she left the relationship, the migraines and arthritis went away.

Psychic or alternative forms of healing such as crystal ball healing are not meant to replace more traditional medicine, although some people choose to let it. There certainly is a time for surgery, for example, and most forms of alternative healing, not only crystal ball healing, are very good for working along with standard western medicine. In fact, scientific western medicine is finally acknowledging the power of alternative methods. Study after study has shown the powerful effect of techniques such as visualization and affirmation, color therapy, music therapy, and energetic healing.

When my second child was born I had to have a sudden emergency operation, because I was hemorrhaging badly. They whisked me over to the nearby operating room, but when they began the procedure, they were in such a hurry that they didn't take the big amethyst crystals out of each hand. While everyone else was worried that I and/or my child would die, I was having a wonderful time! While the operation was going on I "traveled" to a beautiful, twelve-sided room surrounded by archways. Beyond the archways was a brilliant green, but inside the room where I lay on my back, everything, including myself, was a soft violet. While I watched, a circle of twelve violet-robed figures surrounded me, emanating peace, and proceeded to send wave after wave of violet light down my body from head to toe. It was the most indescribable feeling! The waves were like a cross between light and shimmering sound. Each time one went through my body I felt a buzzing, sort of like an electric current, but gentler. As each wave shimmered its way through me I just kept feeling more and more peaceful. I didn't try to figure who these beings were, or if they were figments of my imagination. At that point I didn't care. All I knew was that they were there to help heal me . . . and I accepted it.

You could use my experience as the basis of a wonderful healing meditation. Just gaze into your crystal ball until you're totally focused, then visualize going inside your crystal ball into the twelve-sided violet room. Using the crystal ball to help you focus, visualize yourself lying back, being surrounded by these peaceful beings and being healed.

Sometimes it helps, especially at first, to have someone lead you in the visualization while you gaze into your crystal ball. If you want to do it yourself, you might want to record it and play it back. I've recorded it myself in a cassette called "Healing" that is listed in the last chapter, "Further Resources." No matter the method, it can provide a powerful experience because the crystal ball helps keep you so much more open and focused. Then you're especially open to guidance and the images can impact you in a very meaningful way. I work quite often with guided visualization, crystals, and crystal balls and have always seen how powerfully it can work. You'll find some of these recorded guided visualizations in the resource section of this book.

☺

SETTING GOALS—FINDING OUT
WHAT YOU REALLY WANT TO DO IN LIFE

So much of the time we find ourselves doing things we don't want to do. We may be working in jobs that we had to take, behaving in ways that don't bring us happiness, being buffeted around by the needs of those around us rather than responding to our own needs. Many of us, for one reason or another, are not doing what we want to do but what other people want us to do. Circumstances may have forced us into situations that we dislike, but we stay in them to survive. Sometimes we don't even trust our own perceptions and feelings, especially if they seem to be different from everyone else's. Our behavior, sometimes even our thoughts, are so dictated by cultural, religious, familial, and other forms of conditioning, that it's not surprising so many of us don't know what we want. For one reason or another, we have stilled our own voice so long that we don't even hear it anymore. It hasn't disappeared, though. It's there waiting for us if we can identify it.

This crystal ball meditation can very quickly bring your own voice to the forefront. In identifying your goals, don't worry how you're going to achieve them. You can plan that later. Right now, just identify them. Gaze into your crystal ball and when you are focused, calm, and centered, ask yourself: If I knew I was going to die tomorrow how would I live right now? Don't try to figure out the answer. Instead, free-associate, and answer with the first things that come to your mind. Say them aloud for someone else to hear, or say them into a tape recorder. Keep your attention in the ball, asking yourself over and over again, "If I knew I was going to die tomorrow, what would I do differently right now?" Would you do anything differently than you are doing now? Would you change anything? Are there things in your life that you wish you had done? Are there communications that are incomplete? Let the words flow out as you remain in your trance state, connected to your deeper self.

After the meditation, listen to your tape recording, or have the other person repeat back to you what you said you wanted. These wants may be short term or long term. These wants form your goals. If I wanted to vacation in Hawaii, for example, I made it my goal to do so. State each goal simply so it will be achievable. If we state a goal in such a way that it is hard to understand, how can we possibly follow through on it? Confusion is one way to avoid any serious goal setting.

☯

FINDING MORE MEANING IN LIFE

Have you ever felt your life was kind of empty—that the same things happened over and over again and you were just stuck in a rut? I know as a child I used to feel that way sometimes. I remember feeling very bored at the predictability of the lifestyle I saw about me. Looking around, I'd question myself, "Is this all there is? What's the point? Why am I here?" I was surrounded by unspoken rules. Have you ever felt this way? Most of us have at times and it's such times that can turn us toward anything else that can help us find more. Some of us anesthetize ourselves with alcohol or food and others look for meaning by "trying on" different belief systems. Some of us just get real busy. Then we never have to feel empty. Some of us experience this questioning of purpose so intensely that we experience complete nervous collapse, and others may just get the "blahs." Most of us have had a sense that there is much more to life. Is there?

There is. You don't have to go anywhere or do big, grand things. You just have to look more closely right where you are . . . inside and out. I've had to learn this lesson over and over again. I remember once going to India on a one-way ticket to search for enlightenment. (It was all so dramatic!) As soon as I landed, I knew that I didn't need to be there. I hadn't needed to go anywhere!

I realized that I was living much too superficially, skimming over the surface without noticing what extraordinary treasures lay beneath. What I learned was that by diving beneath the surface, even the most ordinary things become extraordinary. And I learned that you can always dive deeper. Not only is it enlightening and fulfilling, but practically speaking, life gets much more interesting! And you can't find your purpose for living unless you experience life beyond the superficial. Crystal ball gazing is one way to dive beneath the superficial surface of life.

For variety, try this: Gaze into your crystal ball until you are in the trance state. Then, looking into the crystal ball, visualize a day in your life. Remember everything about it, even the most ordinary parts, from the start of your day to its finish. See it in your crystal ball or in your mind's eye, which is opening wider the deeper you gaze. See yourself as you get up, as you get breakfast, as you eat, as you leave your house, and as you do everything in your day. Pay attention to what you'd normally overlook, things that are so mundane that you do them without even thinking about them. If an entire day is too much, choose the morning, or even one hour sometime during the day. As you do it, drift deeper and deeper into the ball, relax. You can let your eyes close or keep them open. Do this without judgment or desire to change anything about what you see. Just notice. The crystal ball will help you focus and remember more and more of the subtle things: the feel of the breeze on your cheek when you ran across the street to catch a cab, the ways you automatically responded to certain situations, the way you were breathing when you were going to sleep. Record twelve of these ordinary things that you see on tape so you can access the information later. When you have done that, leave the crystal ball.

Next, go about your day and notice each one of these twelve things as they recur. If you remember the breeze on your cheek, for example, try to notice the breeze on your cheek as you go about your day. Make this awareness your practice for a week and see what difference it makes. (You might have to put up reminders around you at first so you can remember.) Notice everything you can, from the most obvious to the most subtle actions, feelings, bodily sensations, and other impressions. If you like, record your findings so you can learn from them.

This practice can have amazing results. You'll get so much more from life as even little things start to have significance. Your life, which may have seemed so ordinary, can become extraordinary when even something so simple as the sound of a bird in a tree, the breeze against your skin, or a smile from a stranger can be so interesting. Little things, which before you might have dismissed or failed to notice, begin to offer a wealth of experience and meaning. Big things aren't necessary for you to feel that life is valuable. In a very short time you'll find yourself slowing down as you take the time to notice and experience more. You don't feel as if you have to fill your life with lots of things and activities for it to be interesting. In fact, after a while, so many activities and things begin to take away from life's meaning as you notice how distracting they are. More and more you'll find yourself needing to do less, finding your fulfillment in being rather than doing. Finally, as you find yourself slowing down and noticing more of the ordinary things in life, you'll find yourself at the calm center in the whirlwind of life, and feeling a wonderful sense of fulfillment.

DISCOVERING YOUR LIFE PURPOSE

The Chinese have a saying that goes something like this: "A sure way to go crazy is to try to figure out the workings of karma." According to many spiritual traditions the world over, karma has to do with your purpose for living. You are here in this life because you have unfinished karma. Other traditions say that we're on this earth to learn lessons, to learn to love, to glorify God. Others say that there is no reason for living, life just is. No matter what the explanation, the purpose for living isn't anything that you can figure out. What matters is, what is *your* purpose for living? What larger purpose do you feel you serve by being here on this planet? What work do you think you should be doing? No one can tell you. You have to hear the answers within yourself. Your purpose for living can't be *found* until it's first *revealed*.

That's why when you search for your life's purpose with your crystal ball gazing, it should be done prayerfully. To see your life's purpose is a gift that comes to you as you become more calm, centered, and open, when you become more attuned to the Sacred Spirit and can listen to it within yourself. All this can happen when you crystal ball gaze. It may not come to you right away, but with patience, this realization of your life's purpose will come. It may reveal itself gradually to you over a course of years. Or it may come as a flash of sudden inspiration such as a vision in your "mind's eye," or as a strong impression. It may come when you least expect it, or in a dream. Or it may come to you as an answer to your prayers and seeking.

Some like to gaze into the crystal ball, asking to be shown a vision of their life purpose. As they continue to meditate they may see "pictures" of their life purpose, or receive a strong sense about it.

This is a beautiful crystal ball meditation that I like to do: Gaze into your crystal ball and, when you're focused, feel as if you are entering through the sides of the ball into its very center. Eyes open or closed, feel as if you are sitting cross-legged in the center of the crystal, spine straight and hands on your knees. Imagine, then, that a cool, clear violet light enters through the top of your head to fill up your entire body and radiate outward as far as you can see. As you continue to sit in the violet light, very heartfully, as if you are praying, ask to be shown a guiding vision, a purpose, for your entire life or any part of your life. As you continue to sit in the center of your crystal ball, keep your attention focused on your request, opening yourself to receive an answer. If your concentration wavers, prayerfully ask again that you be shown this guiding vision. Again, open your heart to receive. Be patient, be open and don't be in a hurry. Your answer may not come right away. It may not come for a long while. But it will come.

◉

SELF-EMPOWERMENT

That we have an integrated, balanced healthy sense of self is as important in crystal ball gazing as it is in life. If we are self-empowered, we are able to be open, free to receive whatever life offers, and in crystal ball gazing, free to receive whatever our mind's eye shows us. If we are disempowered, we close down and withdraw into ourselves, unable to perceive or to receive what is offered to us, either in life or in the crystal ball. When we're empowered, we feel secure; disempowered, insecure. If we feel fully empowered, we're happy; disempowered, we're unhappy. To be disempowered is to lose the connection with your inner self.

Most of us recognize the signs of disempowerment when they appear: shame, guilt, feeling ineffectual and unloved. We can feel so unworthy, the voice of our inner self so silenced, that we let people "walk all over us," abuse us, violate our sense of personal integrity. The more disempowered we feel, the more we are angry and dissatisfied. We may even turn against ourselves, get depressed and, in extreme cases, suicidal.

Disempowerment in one form or another is as common a theme in crystal ball reading as it is in life. If you're feeling disempowered, you can't stand up for yourself, you're afraid to express yourself, or you're feeling any of the above symptoms, remember: If you feel disempowered, you made the decision to disempower yourself. As long as you think that others have disempowered you, you have given up your power. Until you take credit for your decision to give away your power, you can't even take the first step toward empowerment.

Now, you may have had good reason to give up your power. Perhaps as a child you couldn't stand up to your father or as an adult you had to back down to save your job. I'm not saying that you should never give up your power, but to be whole you need to reclaim it by saying to yourself that *you* made the decision. The reason isn't important.

I had a client who had a hard time accepting this responsibility. I asked him to gaze into the crystal ball and then to look within and see himself in a situation in which he felt disempowered. He saw a situation at work where he disagreed with his boss.

"My boss wanted to spend all this money on computers when the company just didn't have the money to spend. I should know, I'm the accountant. When I talked to him, though, he wouldn't budge an inch. He didn't even want to hear what I had to say! I guess that I got a little heated, because he told me that I could always leave if I was so unhappy with the decision. So I backed down and shut up."

"Good," I said when he was finished. "Now tell me who disempowered you."

"Why, my boss, of course," he replied. "He made me back down."

I had him gaze into the crystal ball more, and then asked him to review the scene more closely. "Your boss may have set up the conditions that made it expedient for you to back down, but you could have chosen differently. You could have chosen to walk out and lose your job. Look closely into the ball; notice how you feel and what you're thinking."

As soon as I said that he saw what I meant. "You're right. I'm thinking that I'd better be quiet because I don't want to lose my job. I was the one that made the decision!"

That realization, as small as it seemed, started him on the path to reempowerment.

I used to do this meditation with my crystal ball in order to connect more strongly with my inner self. It's a variation of two meditation practices I was given years ago. Gaze into your crystal ball until you're centered, calm, and clear. Still focusing in the ball, say these words to yourself, "I am." Keep repeating them as you gaze deeper and deeper into the sphere. Feel yourself, sense yourself. Now ask yourself this question: "Who am I?" Keeping your attention in the crystal ball so your mind doesn't wander, investigate yourself. What do you consist of? Where are your boundaries? What is a self? Where are you? Investigate yourself. When you are finished, back out of the crystal ball and see if you can keep the new experiences of your Self with you. If you continue with this gazing practice for a length of time, you'll notice yourself becoming stronger, more secure, confident and accepting of yourself. You'll have a sense of personal integrity and boundary.

Here is another excellent meditation to do with your crystal ball. It will help with feelings of unworthiness, shame, guilt, and other emotional and mental states that drive us so often in our disempowerment. Gaze into your crystal ball until you are completely focused and visualize yourself inside feeling the guilt, shame, or any other such painful feeling that you have. What is the incident connected with these feelings? Go backward in your life, letting similar past incidents appear to your mind's eye or in the crystal ball. Go as far back in your childhood as you can remember, gazing into the crystal ball and letting all the painful feelings come up for you. Now, "see" that hurt child and send him or her your love. Imagine that a beautiful golden light floods from your heart into the crystal ball and into the child's heart. As you concentrate more and more deeply into the crystal ball, opening your heart, wave after wave of feeling may come up. As they come up, keep sending your love to that beautiful child who is you.

When I did this meditation what came up for me was forgiveness. In order to send my love I also had to send myself forgiveness ... not for anything specific, but for my very being. It got real heavy. As soon as I was able to do that, though, it got real light! You may find feelings coming up for you that are hard to accept. Accept them all, though, for by doing so you are accepting all the parts of your Self. A lot of the time we think that we have to be perfect. But there is no such perfection. As Jesus said, "Let him who is without sin cast the first stone."

☙

DEVELOPING INTUITION AND PSYCHIC ABILITIES

Most people understand intuition and have been intuitive at least a few times in their lives. Psychism is a different story. Most people don't understand it at all. Being psychic, as mysterious as it may sound, is not abnormal. Everyone is born psychic. Sensitivity to our surroundings and to situations at a distance is a normal human sense. It's there when we're born, but then social conditioning rather emphatically shoves this ability to the background in its emphasis on the physical and rational. This ability doesn't disappear, however; it lies there dormant where social influences have conveniently put it, ready for retrieval.

It's a little like the first days of the telephone. I'm sure, for example, that to most folks the telephone seemed as mysterious then as sending messages telepathically does to us now . . . until they got used to it. But unlike the early telephone that no one had ever used, we do use telepathy and other psychic abilities. It's a fairly common experience, for example, to "just know something" without knowing how you knew. Perhaps you had a "gut feeling" or a hunch. You may not be used to it, but that kind of intuition, more developed, can become psychic ability that will increase with use.

Crystal ball reading automatically increases your intuitive abilities. As you gaze you shift from your rational/logical part of your brain to the intuitive part of your brain. The more you gaze, then, the more you're exercising this intuitive ability, and just like exercising a muscle, the more you use it the stronger it gets. It sounds very mystical, but after a while intuition seems as natural as logic. Artists, musicians, writers, and other creative people use their intuition all the time.

If you would like to be more intuitive, either specifically in your crystal ball gazing or generally in life itself, here are some things that you can do. As I said earlier, wearing crystal ball earposts or earrings puts the crystals closer to your third eye and also stimulates the third-eye energy points on the ear. My jewelry company used to make crystal headbands that would put the crystal right over the third eye. Now we just put a herkimer diamond crystal, a stone that's especially good for the third eye, on a cord, so you can wear it as a headband or a pendant. Be sure to balance it with your grounding and heart-centered spheres. You can do the same thing with a small crystal ball pendant. You can also meditate holding a smaller sphere over your third eye, imagining that a beam of royal blue or indigo light is being sent into it by the sphere in your hand. Every time you inhale, imagine this light is pouring into your third eye, relaxing your forehead and freeing your vision. Hold your charging sphere over your third eye when you gaze to help you open to its vision.

The thing that I've learned about psychism is that it may bring you more information, but it alone can't bring you wisdom. Only when you combine psychism with the love, empathy, compassion, acceptance, and surrender of your heart do you truly have wisdom. Otherwise, the picture is incomplete. That's why all of the practices that I've worked with and all the teachings I have learned tell you not to aim for psychic powers. Rather than concerning yourself with the seeking of psychic powers, it is much better to first seek wisdom. The psychic powers will follow in their own time.

I used to think that gaining more psychic powers and opening my third eye to ever-widening consciousness was the way to reach the Higher Spirit. Looking back, I realize now that I thought of the path as linear, sort of like climbing a ladder. You just kept going higher until you got to the top. My kundalini yoga teacher taught me something different. He used to close my third eye, which would upset me. Here I used to do all this yoga and meditation to get it open, and then he'd close it again! I can still see how he'd look at me, and then slowly, almost with a sense of amusement, ask, "Why do you want it open? What do you intend to do with it? Can you tell me this?" It made me think. I'd meditate on all the things you could do and experience with your third-eye vision. It seemed so exotic, so different, so intriguing, so powerful. But every time I thought of some benefit, I also saw a drawback. For instance, if it made me feel powerful, bolstered my ego, and made me feel I was more special than everyone else. Obviously that wasn't the way! So I never had a good answer to my teacher's questions.

This doesn't mean that you shouldn't use psychic or intuitive or any other type of "power," only that you should consider them from a higher viewpoint. By using them you can break free of limiting beliefs and conditioning about what is possible and real. It is wise, then, if your intuition and psychic abilities develop with your crystal ball gazing, to regard these abilities as teachers, leading you to a larger wisdom and way of being. Balance the psychic work that you do with your open heart, an attitude of service, a healthy respect, and a prayerful attitude.

6

Doorways to Other Worlds

THE "OTHER WORLDS"

There are realms and realms of other realities that exist right along with the physical realm. They each have their separate reality, yet they are also part of each other. What affects one world will, in a ripple effect, affect the others. Yogis, healers, shamans, and metaphysicians have long spoken of at least ten bodies that we have other than our physical and at least ten corresponding worlds that these bodies are part of. Healers, acupuncturists, acupressurists, and others who work with subtle energy, work with at least the etheric body and its subtle energy currents. People who work with sound, color, and visualization affect the astral and mental bodies, which in turn affect the physical body. In crystal ball work, we can learn to operate in and be familiar with all of these other worlds, but the most usual of these to work with are the etheric, the astral, and the mental.

If these worlds are all around us, how come we aren't aware of them? That is because, for the most part, we use only our physical senses, which can only perceive the physical universe. These other worlds require other ways of perceiving in order for us to be conscious of them. Unfortunately, our modern society usually supports the use of only our physical senses. However, it is only when we start using our intuitive mind and stop relying on our physical senses for all our information that we can begin to expand our consciousness to become aware of other realities. These "other worlds" or "planes of consciousness" exist, and you are in them whether you know it or not. However, you can only be aware of them when you have expanded your consciousness sufficiently to experience them.

☺

LIMITLESS AS SPACE

We may identify with our physical body, but actually, when we expand our consciousness and find ourselves in these nonphysical worlds, there is a part of us that continues to exist beyond our physical body. This is what the Buddhists mean when they speak of human beings as being "limitless as space." That part of us that never changes, who we ultimately are, is just awareness, or consciousness itself. It is that part of us that is related to every living being in all of the worlds, physical and nonphysical. Any boundaries we experience are only the result of differing states of consciousness. We are deathless, undying, and limitless. When we crystal ball gaze or use other techniques to let go of our dependence on our physical world, body, and physical senses, we are able to have this experience. Your physical senses, then, connect you with the physical universe and make it real to you. Without them there is no physical universe in your awareness at all.

Likewise, when we don't use our other senses that bring us awareness of these other worlds, these other worlds do not exist to us because we have no way to perceive them. They are real, though, just as real as our physical world, and we can learn to perceive them. As spiritual teachers of all ages and persuasions have long taught, these other senses are lying more or less dormant within us and if we want to be aware of other universes, we have only to switch to another way of perceiving by using these other senses. *As your way of perceiving changes, so does your universe.* So, when we speak of "traveling to other worlds," we don't actually travel anywhere at all, we just change our focus.

As has been illustrated throughout this book, you can use your crystal ball to direct your attention away from your physical body and perceptions and attune yourself to other ways of perceiving. This happens naturally when you gaze and unearth within you your long-buried intuition, your inner voice, and your awareness of subtle energy. The more you use these senses in your crystal ball work, the more you strengthen them. But just because you gaze doesn't necessarily mean that you'll become aware of other planes of consciousness. You need to direct your awareness to them.

☺

THE VALUE OF EXPLORING "OTHER WORLDS"

Why do you want to travel to other worlds? Is it to gain power or to impress other people? Check your motivation before you begin. Be honest with yourself. If your motive is for these kinds of egotistical reasons, it's not going to help. It may even hurt you, because your heart will start closing and your vision will gradually cloud. However, if you go into this area to gain information or to help you serve others, exploration into other worlds can be tremendously helpful. As you will find, there are a lot of benefits, which will unfold as you continue.

As I've mentioned earlier, when you explore other realities your perception expands. As it does, you can see the larger picture surrounding any problem or illness, for example, and so develop even more of an understanding of what to do that will truly help someone. (You'll also know when not to interfere. Sometimes that's the best help of all!)

As in other crystal ball work, the realization of life's relativity helps you to keep your perspective, to lighten up and not drown in your troubles, knowing that the most important things aren't the events in your life anyway. Instead, it's your growing awareness that underlies these events. As in all crystal ball gazing, your perception of who you are shifts as you discover that you are so much more than you thought you were. Your life emphasis shifts from *having* and *doing* to *being*. As you become less attached to life in the same old way, there grows within you a sense of internal freedom and joyfulness.

Ultimately, however, the largest benefit of exploring other realities is that when you are aware of worlds other than the physical, you understand that when you die your awareness doesn't end, because it's not dependent on your physical body, your emotions, or your mental processes. Instead, your awareness is grounded in that central core consciousness that links all planes of reality (different worlds) and continues no matter which world or "reality" dies or is born. In other worlds, something within us is clearly the same all of the time no matter what else changes. With an awareness reaching beyond your physical senses, you realize there is no death, because your awareness continues. Thus present centered, you gain courage in life and are able to hold your own in any circumstance. Instead of apologizing for yourself or holding back in life, you'll feel free to be totally yourself.

☻

OUR OTHER BODIES

Physical bodies only seem solid to us with our physical eyes. Actually, our physical bodies are in a state of constant vibration, as science confirms. According to traditional yoga, the human body is surrounded by ten other bodies, each in its essence, rapidly vibrating particles held together by a certain force: consciousness. They all share this same essence, yet have different characteristics depending on their rate of vibration. For the sake of understanding, these different bodies can be pictured as layers, one on top of each other, even though each body really is contained within the next higher body. In crystal ball gazing we almost always work with three other bodies besides the physical: the etheric, the astral, and the mental. Of these four bodies, the physical has the slowest, most dense, rate of vibration. It can be pictured in the center, with each succeeding body extending outward from it to form roughly an egg shape. As the etheric, then the astral, then the mental body extends outward from the physical, the rate of vibration is faster, finer, and less dense, the mental body being the finest of the four.

THE ETHERIC AND THE MENTAL

The etheric body has no consciousness apart from your physical body. It is the energetic "body double," which includes your chakra (subtle energy) system. In crystal ball gazing, we interact with this body every time we open our heart, for example, ground or center ourselves, or otherwise work with the subtle energy systems. We interact with the etheric body when we wear crystal balls, work with them as charging spheres, or use them for their color.

The other bodies, however, have a reality and consciousness apart from your physical body and physical world. Just as the physical body is part of a larger physical world, the astral body is part of an astral world and the mental body is part of a mental world. Just as a physical world is formed by physical elements, the other worlds are each formed by its own set of elements. The mental world is formed by thought; ours and others. It's made up of mental vibrations which create their own images. This is the realm of telepathy. Often in our crystal ball reading we tune into this plane of consciousness to see the images which we then interpret. Any time that we use visualization, imagination, or any sustained thought, we form an image or "body" in this world. Not only do we influence the mental plane, we are influenced by it. Vibrational emanations from this world, attracted by our receptivity, come to our brains in the form of thoughts. This happens all the time with people. How many times, for example, have you heard people say things like, "This thought just came to me," or "This just flashed into my mind." Because all the physical and nonphysical worlds and bodies are interrelated, the mental world affects the astral, which affects the etheric and physical. So in crystal ball gazing, depending on your strength of focus, you take part in the mental world each time that you concentrate, visualize, or project your thoughts in order to change something in the physical world.

You see evidences of this interaction between these planes of consciousness everyday in "real" life too. Barry Bonds, for example, one of the greatest baseball players today, told a stadium of Little League children and their parents (including me) that he uses visualization all the time to keep improving his hitting. He followed by saying that visualization was so effective that it was almost as important to him as the actual practice. This is a perfect example of what I'm talking about. In this case, when Barry visualizes his hitting, it becomes a thought form on the mental plane, which then embodies itself in the astral world. This embodied event in the astral world, in turn, influences the "reality" in the physical world . . . Barry Bonds hitting the ball. Dreaming, which often takes place on the astral plane with your astral body, is another good example. How many times have you experienced something in a dream and upon awakening find that it has affected your mood?

☺

THE ASTRAL BODY AND THE ASTRAL WORLD

The astral body is somewhat contained within, but also extends beyond, the etheric body. It has a rate of vibration higher than the physical and etheric, but lower than the mental and causal. This body is the vehicle of sensation and emotion. Even if you aren't aware of being in your astral body, you are. You just don't see it. Whenever you express an emotion you are using your astral body, whether you're conscious of it or not. Every feeling and every thought that affects you personally affects and is reflected in this body. Your astral body bridges your physical and mental bodies, responding to that which is directed from them both consciously and unconsciously.

You can consciously inhabit your astral body apart from your physical body. This happens automatically in your sleep, but unless you have built a connection between your astral and physical bodies you will remember very little about it. Your ability to use your astral body apart from your physical body depends on how conscious you are in it. To be conscious in your astral body you need to be able to build a bridge or a connection between that body and your physical body. This is an etheric bridge or connection that allows you to operate in your astral body and remain conscious as you shift back to your physical body. If you are able to do that, you can remember all your experiences and information and can communicate and make use of them in the physical. When this connection is strong and you can remain conscious in your astral body, there exists a continuous stream of consciousness in which there is no difference between states of sleeping and waking, life and death.

Even though there are many "worlds" that you can go to using your crystal ball, the astral world, the world of feelings, dreams, and spirit guides, is probably the one most crystal ball gazers travel to. The astral world is an entire independently existing universe that occupies the same space as our physical universe. All our feelings and associated thoughts register in this world and the ones belonging to you form your own astral body. Though the objects and events in the astral world are shaped and formed by the imagination and thoughts of those on it, it has an independent existence apart from the mind. This world has brilliant, fantastic lights, sounds, and sights that don't exist in the physical world.

Our bodies are even made of light. Perception here is quite different from physical perception and can be confusing until you learn to use your astral senses. Being in the astral world is very much like being in a dream. In fact, many of your dreams are actually astral experiences. Also, sometimes an astral vision can come to you spontaneously, especially during times of intense prayer or contemplation, when you have raised your body's vibrational rate.

❧

ASTRAL AND TIME TRAVEL

When you shift your consciousness between your physical world and the astral world the sensation that you experience is rather like one of travel or movement in space. Here, again, "astral travel" is misleading because, contrary to the "travel" sensation, you really go nowhere since the astral is contained within the physical body. Even though in one sense you don't go anywhere when you astral-travel, you can still travel in the astral world with your astral body. You do this in the same way that you do here in physical life; you use your will, intending to move. If you want to move your arm, for example, it won't move of itself. You have to decide or intend for it to move. Likewise, if you see a mountain in the distance on the astral plane and you want to go to it, just decide to do it and you'll be there. Distance is entirely different on the astral plane, so chances are that as soon as you decide to be there, you will be. You'll find that things are not quite solid in the same way as in your physical life. You can go through walls and other objects and see through things that you normally couldn't. There seem to be no barriers in the usual sense. When you move it's different too. Often you'll have the sensation of gliding, floating, or flying.

When you understand the interrelationship among the different planes of consciousness and how they affect and are affected by each other, you have another way to understand how you can "see" or time-travel into the past or the future: If all objects, thoughts, emotions, events, etc., on the physical plane first manifest on the subtle planes (i.e., the astral, mental, causal, etc.), then when you're "seeing" into the future, you are actually sensing or "seeing" that subtle plane vibration and interpreting the physical plane event that is to follow from it. You will be accurate to the extent that other subtle causes don't intervene. Likewise, anything that has occurred on the physical plane leaves its impression in the subtle planes, recorded in the form of vibration. Cause and effect move in both directions. When you are "seeing" into the past, you are "seeing" this latter vibrational pattern. When you are "seeing" the past or the future, then you are just sensitizing yourself to and interpreting the vibrational or psychic "shadows" which precede and follow physical plane events. From this perspective, then, rather than going anywhere when you time-travel, you just project your awareness on one of the subtle planes of consciousness (usually the astral) and focus on whatever time period you are interested in.

There is another way to understand time travel. At its heart, the movement of time is illusory, merely a logical notion supported by the action and reaction of events. If your complete awareness is entirely centered in the present moment, you are in a place where all time is *now* because there's no movement, no coming and going, no action and reaction that supports the illusion of time. All time is contained there . . . and there's no time at all. It is from this awareness that we can project ourselves through time because the notions of past and future have no more reality.

☺

CRYSTAL BALL GAZING
FOR ASTRAL CONSCIOUSNESS

You can train yourself to become awakened to self-conscious activity on the astral plane using, among other things, crystal ball

gazing techniques, dreamwork, yoga, intense prayer, or meditation. The following is a guided crystal ball gazing technique that
will enable you to shift your consciousness from the physical to the
astral. Actually, you will be making your way around the physical
plane in your astral body.

1. Using the gazing techniques that have already been described,
   enter into your crystal ball. Once you are inside your crystal
   ball, continue to maintain your concentration and visualize
   yourself becoming luminous as you focus on the top of your
   head. As you fill yourself completely with golden light, feel
   yourself growing lighter and lighter, so light that you begin to
   rise to the top of the crystal ball, leaving through its top.

2. See yourself in your mind's eye rising up to the top of the
   room. Look down and find your body. See the luminous cord
   that stretches between you and your body, connecting you.
   Keep practicing until you can do it easily.

3. Once you can easily float out through the top of the crystal
   ball and see your body, look around at the objects in the room,
   then see if you can "fly" your body around the room. Use your
   will to do it. Practice moving your body from side to side and
   up and down. Roll it over from back to front and front to
   back. See your connecting cord stretching thinner and longer
   as you put more space between your bodies.

4. Once you are skilled at moving around the room, leave it.
   You'll notice that you don't have to go through the door, but
   can simply pass through the wall. In the astral world you can
   pass through any object or person, travel any distance, and
   even jump over mountains, depending on the strength and
   focus of your will. Leave the building you're in and travel
   around the neighborhood. Notice every sound, object, person,
   and event that is happening around you in as much detail as

possible and will yourself strongly to remember them. (This will help you remember your experience when you return to your physical body and further strengthen the connection between your bodies.)

5. After you have become thoroughly familiar with the use of your thought and will in your out-of-body experiences around your neighborhood, choose a place anywhere on this planet and transport yourself to it. You'll discover that you can go there instantaneously. Lower your astral body to the ground and walk around, observing, listening, and exploring. Hear the thoughts and feel the emotions of other beings in that location. With your astral senses you'll be especially sensitive to things on subtle levels. You won't be noticed at all unless someone is particularly sensitive. (Dogs, cats, and other animals will usually sense your presence before people will!)

6. At any point during these travels that you're ready to come back to the physical, just use your will to bring yourself back over the top of your crystal ball, see your physical body beneath you, then slowly settle yourself down through the top of your sphere until you are inside. Then exit the way you came in. Before you leave the room, be sure that you're well grounded.

Using this technique you can gain a lot of experience using your astral body and will be able to travel out-of-body anywhere on this physical planet. Once you are comfortable doing it, then you are ready to move up into the astral plane. How do you get there? The same way that you got yourself around out-of-body in the physical plane realm. Shift your awareness and will your focus.

☺

ASTRAL GUIDES AND ASTRAL SHELLS

As you move into the astral plane, it is strongly advisable at first to have a guide with you to acquaint you thoroughly with all its aspects. According to the ancient teachings there are advanced beings on the astral (and other) planes who are specifically there to help those who come there after they die. They will help anyone who is ready. All you have to do is ask. If you ask for guidance and no guide appears for you, you are probably not ready to work on the astral plane. Perhaps your physical body or mental/emotional structure isn't well prepared. Perhaps your motives for wanting to work on the astral plane need to be clarified. Don't worry, be patient. When the time is right, a guide will appear for you if you keep asking.

There are a few things to keep in mind about someone who offers to guide you: Just because a being is on the astral plane doesn't mean that they're more advanced, more conscious than you, or in some way special. You're not necessarily more conscious just because you don't have a physical body. After all, people leave their bodies every time they die and move through the astral plane. A being may be drawn to you by the force of your own desire and actually have little or nothing to offer you even if they offer to help. They may have the all-too-human tendency to lie to you, try to impress, or play tricks on you. Or they may actually be detrimental to your efforts. Some of these beings are actually just astral bodies whose inhabitants have already departed, their consciousness in other worlds. Left alone, this body's astral form will disintegrate unless it is kept "alive" (in form) by the lingering thoughts of its prior owner or by the thoughts of those on the physical plane who think they're in contact with a being, thoughts which keep the body in movement and form so it seems alive. Any speech of this body is actually just the reflection of the consciousness or subconsciousness of those who are empowering it with their thoughts. If you draw one of these "shells" to you, the more you interact with it and accord it beingness, the more it seems to speak. Really, though, there's nobody home.

If you meet a nonphysical guide or other being who offers to help, how do you know if it's the real thing? Evaluate him or her the same way that you would someone on the physical plane. What is your gut feeling? Do you experience a sense of harmony with them? Do they feel right in your heart and do their teachings line up with your sense of inner truth? Don't get caught up in their appearance (which will usually be pleasing to you) or their personality. Those things aren't really important. It's the teachings that you want to pay attention to.

If you ever meet a nonphysical being that you feel afraid of, or if you ever feel any fear for any reason, just open your heart and send out love. Love is the strongest force there is and can vanquish anything.

☻

MEETING ANGELS, SPIRIT GUIDES, AND TEACHERS

Just as when you ask for an astral guide, a teacher or helper will appear when you are ready. They don't even have to appear in dramatic visions or in mystical circumstances. You don't have to astral-travel or crystal ball gaze. Actually, guides, angels, and other helpers are all around us. We just need the "eyes" to see them. They don't always appear as we expect them to, either, so often we miss them entirely, even if they are calling out to us. Your orientation is important too. If you want to meet a spiritual guide, an angel, or another helper, keep yourself attuned to the Higher Spirit. In the words of an old yoga teaching, "A pickpocket, when meeting a great saint, only sees his or her pockets." If we expect an angel to be floating in the sky, female, golden-colored, with big wings, a long skirt, and a round halo over her head, as we see in pictures, for example, if she doesn't look like that we probably won't even see her.

An angel, guide, or spiritual teacher may also have no form at all. If you ask to meet a guide when you are crystal ball gazing and only hear an inner voice instead of seeing a body, you might not realize that your guide is there and talking to you. How do you know when you've met an angel or felt its presence? You can feel it. It's pure love, unconditional and total acceptance. Joy. You may not see the body of the angel, for example, but if you're attuned, you can feel its presence. You may feel the angelic presence in nature, in music, in art, or in the everyday events of life. You may see it shining out of the eyes of a stranger, or your friend, your child, or your mate. You may feel its presence within yourself if you're quiet and openhearted.

☺

CRYSTAL BALL GAZING TO MEET
AN ANGEL, SPIRIT GUIDE, OR TEACHER

Here is a crystal ball gazing technique that you can use to call an angel, guide, spiritual teacher, or any other helper to you:

1. Gaze into your quartz crystal sphere until you are "inside," totally concentrated, relaxed, and grounded. Let yourself feel very peaceful.

2. Now, in your mind's eye, notice that there is light surrounding you. See it as clear, bright, golden light. Ask the Higher Spirit to protect you during this meditation, that no harm and only the highest good should come to you.

3. While still inside this glowing orb of light, feel a softening in your center and let your heart open. Visualize your heart as a green glow edged in pink . . . very soft and very clear. Extend this light out from your heart center so that it forms a path . . .

green edged in pink. This path extends further and further out in front of you as you open and relax.

4. Now invite an angel, a guide, a teacher, or any being that you like to come and be with you. See it in the distance and invite it with all your heart into the green glow with you. In all love and openness, welcome that being into your heart.

5. Now see that being come toward you on the green/pink path extending from your heart. As you watch, it comes close and closer until it is before you. As it approaches you, it too becomes filled with the green glow. Like you, it feels open, soft, and trusting. Welcome this being.

6. Breathing in and out of your heart center, begin to communicate with it. If you run out of words or don't know what to say, use your feelings. Don't hesitate to ask any question. Be open. Trust. Love and let go, leaving nothing unsaid or hidden. Don't be in a hurry. Communication from them can come in many forms, as images, as words or as a feeling inside. Listen and be aware. Don't dismiss any input that comes to you. If you like, you can ask it how to be contacted in the future or how you will know it if it appears to help you in everyday life.

7. When you are through, or it seems like time to go, bid it farewell and thank it. Watch it back away from you along the green/pink pathway that extends from your heart, growing smaller and smaller until you no longer see it. Hold the feeling of it in your heart.

8. Now bring your consciousness back to your heart, feeling it as soft and open. Know that you are loved. As you feel this, slowly pull the green/pink glowing pathway of light back toward your heart, pulling the light in . . . in . . . in . . . until there's no more path and all the light fills your heart.

9. Keeping your heart open, bring your attention back to the

golden orb of light that surrounds you. Bring this light into your body, relaxing and filling yourself with peace as you become filled with light.

10. See the quartz crystal around you, then slowly back out of it, retaining the loving feeling inside of you and remembering your communication as you come back to "regular" consciousness.

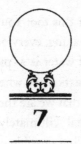

7

Keep Your Feet on the Ground

"If I speak with the eloquence of men and of angels, but have no love, I become no more than blaring brass or crashing cymbal. If I have the gift of foretelling the future and hold in my hand not only all human knowledge but the very secrets of God, and if I also have that absolute faith which can move mountains, but have no love, I amount to nothing at all. If I dispose of all that I possess, yes even if I give my own body to be burned, but have no love, I achieve precisely nothing."

St. Paul i Corinthians

UNITY

In all these "worlds," whether the physical, the astral, or the mental, you're still yourself, a center of awareness, the awareness that is the same in all worlds. And that is what is important, no matter what plane of reality you're focusing on. I finally stopped trying to figure out which "world" I was functioning in when I was crystal ball gazing and decided just to enjoy the experiences from the viewpoint of that center of awareness as much as possible. This doesn't mean that I don't think about what I'm experiencing. I just try to keep myself open to any experience. Ultimately, it's from that center of awareness, that central unity, that I'll find my deepest understanding ... whether it's with crystal gazing or life in general.

When you experience yourself as being the center of awareness, it's important to remember this too: You aren't the only center of awareness. Figuratively speaking, every one of us is a piece of that awareness just as a drop of water is a "piece" of an ocean. This is what the ancient spiritual texts mean when they say that the entire universe lies within us and that we are the entire universe. There is an essential unity that is real. Ultimately, it is this essential unity that makes crystal ball reading possible.

The Reverend (and ex-Bishop) James Pike expresses this very succinctly in the book *Psychics*, when he says, "I now think there's a relationship with all facets of life, a larger unity that we don't fully grasp, and that ordinary methods of measurement and ordinary limitations are transcended." He adds that if we can understand whatever is going on in any area, we can better use it in other areas of life. "If there's something to the synchronicity concept of the late Dr. Jung, if there's something to the collective unconscious, if there's something to a universe in which everything is involved and tied together, and if time and space are limiting concepts only to our conscious minds and maybe not to reality as such—then certainly there is room left for things like palmistry, numerology, astrology and other psychic phenomena." And crystal ball gazing as well.

Within that unity, differences are just as real . . . and just as important. However, one difference isn't any better or worse than any other. There is a difference between a leaf on a tree, a rock, an animal, and a person. There is a difference between water, air, and fire. There are differences between people. So to be in balance, to "see" the whole picture, both the essential unity and the differences within that unity need to be acknowledged. No two snowflakes are alike, for example, yet when they're melted they are all water. Each person is totally unique, yet we all share the same basic biochemical elements. Astral bodies are different from physical bodies, yet they both vibrate. The yin/yang symbol expresses this perfectly: Yin and yang are each separate, yet each is also contained in the other, together forming a unity. To think of yin as better than yang, or of the astral plane as being more special than the physical, is to miss their unity. Likewise, to think of yourself as superior is to miss the point. Is a rock any more special than a tree? Are you any more special than your brother?

☺

A TRUE LIFE LESSON

Besides thinking that you're superior, you can easily fall into the trap of thinking that your experience in other worlds is more important than experience in the physical world. As soon as you've made this distinction, you've again forgotten that they are really one and the same, forgotten the unity of all forms of being and planes of consciousness. In this way, crystal ball gazing can be like the best TV in the world, making it easy to withdraw from life, especially if you have a difficult life or want more excitement. If you decide that other worlds are more important than the physical one, real life can hardly compare! Like TV, it lures you in.

I had experience with some of these mistakes myself some years back when I was living in a yoga ashram in Los Angeles (the one I talked about earlier). I was meditating for hours a day, going off into "other worlds" so often that after a while they seemed more real to me than "real" life. What could be more important than sailing among the stars, meeting nonphysical spiritual beings and other such things? Regular life seemed mundane and unimportant. I stopped doing my part of the housekeeping, cooking, and other daily chores of ashram life. I rationalized it by thinking that no one else in the ashram was doing what I was doing, so they should take over my part. Not only that, but I had claimed the only room to stay in that wasn't filled with other people, believing that I deserved it because what I was doing was more important than what anyone else was doing.

My conceit was not appreciated by the others, and they eventually complained to my teacher about my lack of participation. He called me in to see him, and after questioning me, he moved me into a room with six other women and gave me double the jobs to do that I had in the first place. At first I was astounded. How could he do this to me when I was doing such important work!

Eventually I understood. What I was doing wasn't more important than what anyone else was doing, nor was I by doing it. Cleaning and cooking was just as important work, as was helping others to be more comfortable so they could do theirs. We were all an equally important part of a larger whole. This part of life, the everyday, was just as important as my meditations. These other, nonphysical, worlds aren't any more or less important than the physical world, as fascinating as they may be.

☺

DENIAL AND DISASSOCIATION

My time in the ashram taught me another thing about balance that I find as important in my crystal ball gazing as I do in general. I was meditating so much that I was acutely aware of the relative nature of this physical life. Physical reality seemed much less important and I ignored it because I so clearly knew that it wasn't the only thing there was. This attitude, too, is imbalanced, a form of denial and escape. The idea isn't to leave this world behind, but to have a foot in both the physical and the nonphysical.

Whether in crystal ball gazing or life in general, the dynamic is the same. Instead of "seeing" more, you're actually "seeing" less if you disassociate from yourself and your own thoughts and feelings, denying them with the excuse that "they're not real." Likewise, in crystal ball work, don't use what you "see" in the crystal ball as an escape to avoid your own feelings and thoughts, or to trivialize the importance of your everyday life. It should help with your life, not take you away from it.

Just because you know that physical life isn't everything is not an excuse for lazy or passive behavior. We're here for a reason. We still have responsibilities in life, to ourselves, to others, and to the purpose for which we were born. Live in the heavens . . . and still earn your living! This is the way of the householder yogi and the spiritual path of the Sikhs. As the great Indian saint (and my teacher), Neem Karoli Baba, used to say, "To be truly enlightened is to be balanced on all planes."

SELF-DECEPTION

When you experience some of these other states of consciousness they can be so seductive that you entirely lose your perspective. (This truth holds equally for all metaphysical and spiritual work.) Instead of maintaining your awareness of the larger picture, you get caught in the web of your own ego and your own desires. It's a necessary part of all metaphysical and spiritual work to take some precautions against self-deception, not only because it's detrimental for your growth in awareness, but because it can also be harmful to others. Take precautions even if you think that you don't need to. In fact, if you don't think that you need to take precautions, because you're more developed or for whatever other reason, you probably especially need to take them!

EGO-TRIPPING

In any metaphysical or spiritual work, it is possible to end up on one huge ego trip that is very difficult to escape. If you open yourself up to undesirable influences such as greed, self-importance, and power-tripping, they'll only be magnified the more you use the crystal ball. It's easy to impress people, especially if they're gullible. It's easy to use your reading to one-up someone you're working with, to feel superior, or to get something from them—"fan worship," sex, money, glamour—the works. This strategy will backfire, sometimes to horrible effect. To make the matter worse, often you're not even conscious of what you are doing and you are blinded by your own subconscious needs. Crystals are often tremendous amplifiers of energy, so, as I've said before, what you put in you'll get back—severalfold. If you fall for the ego trip, you'll eventually sacrifice yourself, your integrity, and eventually your own self-respect and the respect of others. *It's not worth it!*

When you get caught thinking you're superior in any way, or get too impressed with experiencing other states of consciousness, it is a sign that you're being blinded and you aren't as aware as you think that you are. And as long as you hold that limiting viewpoint, your blindness is increasing. Then, instead of increasing your awareness and ability with every reading, they are actually diminishing. Energetically speaking, as soon as you think of yourself as special, unique, or different, you start separating yourself from the larger consciousness and your upper chakras (heart, third eye, throat, and crown) start closing. This further decreases your awareness. The Hindu scriptures speak of this as "falling into delusion." This process will negatively affect your crystal ball gazing and your entire life. Instead of "lightening up" and feeling a sense of inner peace, fulfillment, and inner spaciousness, then, you begin to experience the opposite. Striving to satisfy your own needs, you'll lose your sense of compassion, empathy, and heartful connection with people. With your upper energy centers closing, you'll start to lose any psychic or other abilities that you had gained by crystal ball gazing. Practically speaking, your readings will start to lose their accuracy.

☺

MAKING THINGS UP

Fabrication is another trap that you can easily fall into, especially if you're insecure, trying to impress people, or using your crystal ball to earn a living . . . all situations that make you feel as if you have to come up with a vision when you may not have one.

As John Godwin, in his book *Occult America*, describes: "Then come money, fame and the thrill of having a huge audience hanging breathlessly on every utterance. And with it the demand for more glimpses . . . more details . . . specific details—minute details. . . . Like the goose that has laid the golden egg, the augur has to keep on laying to hold the attention of that admiring multitude. It can't be done, because the gift doesn't work that way. So the seer learns to embroider visions, to magnify and finally to invent them altogether. And the more he or she fabricates, the more oblique and generalized he has to become in order to give them at least an average chance of fulfillment. From being a seer he deteriorates into a mere calculator of odds, laboring frantically to keep up with the clamor."[1] This is what happens when you're desperate.

This trap gets really subtle too. It's easy to convince yourself that a half-truth or embroidery "isn't that bad," and then one leads to another. You can even convince yourself that what you're seeing is real, rather than your own fabrication, especially if you keep things general enough. This is what happens when your ego gets involved. Instead of having to come up with "visions on demand," it's best to be able to bide your time until you truly see something or until you're not tempted to color your seeing with your own ideas and prejudices. Sometimes it's best not even to put yourself in the situation of having to come up with something on a regular basis. Keep yourself in the position of having it be okay for you not to see anything.

1. John Godwin, *Occult America*. Garden City, NY: Doubleday & Company, 1972; p. 89.

◡

POWERS

Many of the ancient teachings warn over and over about the danger of having "powers." Psychism, clairvoyance, the abilities to travel in time and on the astral plane, and others that can come to us from crystal ball gazing are some of these powers that they are talking about. In fact, as I explained earlier, some teachings warn you to avoid any powers at all because of their inherent dangers in leading you astray and warn how easy it is to mistake the powers for the source of the vision itself. They advise that you ignore them if they come to you, and certainly not to seek them, advising that, instead, you focus on the essence that is contained within them.

However, when you do any of this type of work, whether it be crystal ball gazing, meditation, yoga, or prayer, it is almost inevitable that you will develop in these ways and have powers, so it's extremely important to hold them in the proper context. The thing to remember is what has been explained many times in the pages of this book—the crystal ball helps reveal an inner wisdom that every one of us already possesses. Powers are merely a by-product of our attunement with that inner wisdom. You are not superior to anyone else and you're not doing anything that can't be done by anyone given the proper training and perspective. *To be impressed by powers is to lose the sight of their source.* All you've done is learn how to access this wisdom. Remember, it's very easy to impress others and yourself with abilities that may seem amazing on their face. So watch out! Also, it helps to hold on to some healthy skepticism. Many times, to take myself off the pedestal that clients may want to put me on, I demystify them, explaining the (very natural) mechanics of what I do, how I'm able to do it, and how they can do it themselves.

☻

MANIPULATION

When you are very intuitive or can "see" psychically, more often than not you'll know exactly what to say or do to get exactly what you want, so it's easy to be manipulative . . . and then justify it by saying to yourself that "it's all for their own good" or some other such rationalization. That's hard to get out of, because everyone around you is telling you what a wonderful person you are, reinforcing you instead of seeing the real dynamic. Consider this, for example: You want a raise and you psychically see in your crystal ball that your boss is having trouble with his son at home. So you start buying him books on child raising, telling him over and over what a good father he is and how wrong his son is, and sure enough, you get the raise. The problem is, that even though you seem to be helping the boss, really what you want is the raise. That's manipulative. Your fellow employees may even unknowingly reinforce your manipulation by telling you what a wonderful person you are to care so much about your boss! You may not even realize your dishonesty yourself.

☻

OTHER SIGNS OF GETTING OFF-TRACK

If you find yourself getting defensive, especially if someone questions you about your accuracy, something's not right. Often it's because they struck a nerve. Question yourself. Take another look at what they're saying. Is any part of it true? Does it touch upon something else that you're avoiding? Whether there is any truth to what they're saying or not, you've moved away from a true understanding of your essential self. You can start getting back on track by asking yourself this question, "Where is the self that I'm defending?"

As I explained earlier, one sign that you're off balance in some way is that you start getting sick or you're tired all the time. This may just mean you're overworked or your nervous system is overtaxed. It could also be a sign of something else more fundamentally out of balance. Finally, if things in your life seem all out of sync, if nothing goes right, this may be a sign of disharmony somewhere in your life. Something is blocking the flow of energy. Now, this could be because you have some life lesson to learn, but generally speaking, when you are aligned with the Higher Spirit, you're in alignment with a certain life flow. Again, investigate yourself honestly. Check your motivations and your actions. Are they in harmony with the Higher Spirit and with your own internal sense of truth?

LOOK TO YOUR PURPOSE

The most important thing about crystal ball gazing is that it can arouse within you the sure knowledge and experience that there is something beyond this physical world and its phenomena. To do crystal ball reading just to be able to astonish your friends isn't much of a purpose at all. What is your purpose? Look into your heart, and if you believe you may be of more service to humanity, then learn to crystal ball gaze and develop yourself. Now, that doesn't mean that you shouldn't go into it if you're curious. Curiosity leads to discovery and learning.

You don't need to be "spiritual" to do this either. However, as you begin to see past the blinders of your physical senses, you'll find a natural spirituality developing in your life. If nothing else, you'll find it in a certain open-mindedness and excitement about the possibility of being led into deeper meanings of life. And I think that a sense of spirituality is very valuable because it will help you with your integrity. Without basic integrity, compassion, and empathy, the temptation to gaze just for yourself, hurting others in the process, is high. Without integrity to guide you, there is such potential for misuse and harm that I would urge leaving crystal ball gazing alone.

❧

AVOIDING OR ESCAPING THE TRAPS

To guard against the improper use of the crystal ball, many of the ancient methodologies had elaborate prayers and rituals that had to be followed. In the words of an old French Cabbalistic manuscript: "Those who desire to establish communication with the good spirits of the crystal must lead a religious life and keep themselves unspotted from the world. The operator must make himself clean and pure, using frequent ablutions and prayers for at least three days before he attempts to practice. . . ."[2] Though it's not necessary to pray for three days before doing a reading, some precautionary practices (like the ones in this book) will make your reading that much more powerful and will keep you aligned with the Higher Spirit.

As I said before, a teacher can stop you if you veer off-track. Whether you have a teacher or not, knowing the traps can help you avoid them or escape and move on. Generally speaking, the right attitude is important. In crystal ball gazing (and in life itself), it will help you stay on course if you follow these ten rules:

THE TEN RULES

1. *Don't take yourself too seriously.* Be able to laugh at yourself and retain a sense of "divine humor."

2. *Be thankful.* Remember that ultimately everything is a gift from the Higher Spirit. Your increasing awareness, for example, doesn't mean you are more deserving or that you've worked harder. Ultimately, it's simply grace.

2. Athene Williams et al, *The Fortune Tellers.* New York: Black Watch, 1974; pp. 82–84.

3. *Be humble.* Someone who is truly humble doesn't call people's attention to it. Truly humble people aren't even aware that they're humble. This kind of humility comes from having a sense both of your place in the essential unity in life and also of divine grace. Don't make a big deal out of what you're doing and experiencing, because not only is it a gift, it's all in the natural order of things.

4. *Don't teach anyone who hasn't asked you for it.* Anytime that you decide that someone needs teaching, you are being presumptuous. You're probably also covering up your own insecurities. By deciding to teach someone, whether it's about crystal balls, the information you see in them, or something that you think will "improve" the other person, you're making the decision that you know more than they do or that you're somehow better. If they're not strong within themselves, your "teaching" can create a co-dependent relationship that merely feeds both of your egos. If you're on the receiving end of this and have awareness, it can be annoying. Also, once you designate yourself as a teacher, it's hard to avoid the tendency to be "perfect," not admitting any flaws in yourself, and causing ever-increasing pressure and stress. So if you see something in your crystal ball that you decide you should teach to someone else, no matter how much you think that they need it, resist the temptation. You can share information, however, if it is appropriate that you do so. You can share without "teaching."

5. *Don't judge.* Judging is another form of one-upmanship. The more you judge, the more you increase your separation from the central, unifying awareness. As Jesus said, "Look not for the speck in someone else's eye, look for the log in your own." The thing to remember is this: In order even to recognize the thing that you're judging, it has first to be somewhere in yourself. So, each time that you judge someone, you are equally as "guilty" as the one judged.

6. *Be discerning.* To be nonjudgmental doesn't mean that everything is always okay. It's not a prescription for "anything goes." You can still use discernment or insight, distinguishing what people or behaviors are helpful or right for you. You can withhold judging a thief, for example, without condoning his or her behavior. Likewise, you don't have to be a doormat just because you're nonjudgmental. Judgment, as opposed to discernment, is a much more personal evaluation of the *worthiness* of a person. It is also a way to make yourself "right" at someone else's expense. Discernment, however, springs from observation. There is a big difference. As I spoke about earlier, be discerning in your communications, during your readings, and also in the rest of your life. Know when it would be more harmful to say something to someone, for example, than to not say it.

7. *Don't cause harm with your speech, thoughts, or actions.* In order to deliberately harm someone, you have to close your heart and block off your sense of empathy and compassion. Not only is this injurious to your own happiness, but it will close you off to any awareness of the higher planes of reality. Most of the time, when people think of not causing harm, they just think about their actions. However, your speech can cause just as much, if not more, pain as any physical action. Gossip harms people too, affecting others' opinions of them and thus their future interrelationships. If confidentiality is important and you violate that, you are violating the trust someone had of you. Improper thoughts can cause harm to you as well as others. Thoughts create realities, not only physical but in the subtle planes. If you have harmful thoughts, you affect yourself emotionally, which then has physical results. It's not unusual, for example, to think so many angry thoughts that you make yourself sick. Someone else can be affected by your thoughts too. This is especially true if you have developed the ability to concentrate your mind, because you may uncon-

sciously project harmful thoughts upon another. If you find yourself having harmful thoughts, instead of dwelling on them, observe them and, as they come to your attention, just let them go.

8. *Instead of being* self-*serving, be* other-*serving.* When you do your crystal ball gazing and other spiritual or metaphysical work, and when living life itself, do it in the attitude of service. Even if you are doing the work to benefit yourself, also dedicate it to the higher good, to the benefit of all mankind, remembering that we are all related. Know that each time that any one of us raises our consciousness to any degree, it affects all beings in all realms. Take the process beyond the automatic, however, and make it a conscious decision. This orientation will take you safely beyond the desires of your ego, steer you away from inflated ideas of self-importance, and keep you focused on the larger picture. You'll find more happiness from serving than from trying to get things for yourself. This attitude is so important that in some traditions it is said to be, in itself, an entire path to the Higher Spirit.

9. *Be honest with yourself and others.* Be honest in your actions, your speech and in your observations. Honesty and dishonesty have such far-reaching effects that it can truly be said that without honesty you have nothing . . . and you are truly and completely blind without any hope of recovering your sight unless that honesty is restored. Your own integrity is precious.

10. *Keep a beginner's mind.* It's tempting sometimes to *pretend* that you know something that you don't, or to *assume* that you know it. As soon as you adopt either of these attitudes you close your mind to any other possibilities and all learning is impossible. This irritating and superior attitude will distance you from other people as well. You'll never be able to know all that there is to know! Keep an open mind, what Zen practitioners call the

"beginner's mind," always open to new understandings. There are layers and layers of increasingly subtle information that are available to you if you continue to have the "eyes" to see, the "ears" to hear, and the mind to understand. We are always students, even the best teachers among us.

☙

BURNOUT

I have spoken about balance throughout this book. Here is another very important part of maintaining balance that you'll need to pay special attention to, especially if you end up doing lots of crystal ball gazing work. I'll start by telling you a story about what happened to me about ten or eleven years ago:

I'd never been very good at saying no to people. Now I see that I should have been. I was lying in bed, with hardly the strength to move, trying to breathe without coughing. My lungs were burning and my chest felt as if it were bound with tight iron bands, every breath a struggle. It was my second round of bronchial pneumonia in three months. I wasn't surprised that I'd caught it again so soon after I'd supposedly recovered. I was tired . . . bone-tired . . . exhausted.

I had been traveling around the country giving crystal workshops, running my crystal-jewelry business, writing, and composing, while still trying to have as normal a home life for my children as possible. To say that I was busy was an understatement. I had a lot of energy then, so I was able to do it.

Then the crystal craze started. I'd been working with crystals and stones for years as well as showing other people how to do it, but it had always been low-key until now. Like an explosion, suddenly, it seemed everyone wanted to work with crystals. And I was delighted! I saw it as more than a fad, but as a leap of consciousness for mainstream America. Years back, I'd been teaching yoga and meditation for a while, hoping to be able to do something to help people be happier and more conscious, but it was frustrating because its appeal seemed limited to "alternative" folks. (At that time yoga and meditation weren't as popular as they are today.) I had been looking for a way to introduce some of these practices more into the mainstream when suddenly one day I realized that if people worked with crystals and stones they'd have to meditate and do some yoga, because that's what it took to work with the stones. How else could you ground and center yourself, learn to focus, and have the necessary consciousness? Once people worked with the stones, their consciousness would expand. I had no idea at the time that I first started talking about it that so many people would get involved.

But I loved it! It seemed as though consciousness in America was going through a major shift and I was part of it. What a way to do some good! How wonderful to be able to help! Every time that I put on a workshop and saw a roomful of people meditating because of the crystals, I got marvelously happy. I was excited . . . and running on a high. It was like riding the crest of an enormous wave with extraordinary power underneath that just swept me forward.

If I could just keep my balance. That was the hardest part, because it was so demanding. Part of the reason was that more and more people asked me to do things. "People need a book!" So I'd write a book. "Design some more crystal jewelry!" So I'd design the jewelry. "This person needs a crystal healing session, and this one too, and this one, and this one. . . . " Write this article . . . speak at this gathering . . . and by the way, design some more jewelry. All this I'd do. And then, I had so many ideas myself, none that could wait for later. I'd think how nice it would be for people to have guided visualization tapes and meditation music, for example, so I made them. And then there were the everyday things. "Oh, can you pick the kids up from school, make dinner, answer the phone?" "By the way, the plumber's coming this morning. Can you be there?" You have the idea. I was busy!

But I loved it and kept it all balanced. I tried to focus on one thing at a time, and give it my *full* focus at the time. I practiced keeping my equanimity no matter what the situation, figuring that it was a good practice, sort of like being the calm center in the middle of a whirlwind. I also used my yoga and meditation to help . . . and the stones.

It all seemed to be working fine until I started ignoring how I felt, ignoring the warning signs that I wasn't keeping it up as much as I thought I was. I was getting tired. As I said, I had a hard time saying no. If someone needed me, I put their needs first . . . always. So even if I was tired, for example, I'd carry on, rationalizing it by saying things like, "Oh well, I know how awful they feel, and I can rest later." If I felt drained or weak, for example, I knew the yoga or breathing practices to keep me going. It was always "later" for me and "right now" for everyone else and everything else that I "had" to do. Then I started getting sick. It started with colds, then flu, then other illnesses. But I found that I could use my stones to heal these things and keep going. I still wouldn't stop. Then my moods started changing. Instead of equanimity I started feeling edgy, out of sorts. As my needs remained unmet I started feeling resentment. But I ignored it, assuming that I was just losing perspective, being unspiritual or that it would just pass and then I'd be okay.

Now, I'm not advocating that one should be selfish or that it's bad to put others' needs first. On the contrary, it's a wonderful quality. However, what I had forgotten was that there needs to be a balance. You can't keep giving out energy without recharging yourself. As much as you nurture others, you need to nurture yourself. Your feelings are there to tell you something. There is a message in resentment and in edginess. My resentment should have told me that I couldn't keep ignoring my feelings of being tired, for example. If I had really been paying attention to my edginess, I would have started to see that my nervous system was beginning to collapse.

What happened was that I got sick. It started out with yet another cold, and when I didn't rest, I developed a cough. I gave myself a couple of days, grossly underestimating the amount of rest that I really needed, did a lot of practices to get my energy up, and finally had to give up and get a strong cough syrup. However, by that time I couldn't sleep because of the cough. Foolish as I was, I still struggled up to do the crystal work and other things that were "so important." Finally, one morning I couldn't get up. Total collapse! As it turns out, I had a raging case of bronchial pneumonia. I also knew that I had a very weak nervous system and an immune system in near ruin. It was an effort to move, to breathe, to live. Finally, I just gave up and let go. I had no choice but to give myself permission to rest, something that I should have done a long time before.

It took a few months to get my strength back. But that was good, because besides giving me the rest I needed, it also gave me time to think about what had happened. Looking back, I realized that I had ignored every warning sign in spite of all the instructions I had received about them. I saw the imbalance in the way I had been living. It's like basic wiring; if you load up too much energy on one circuit, you're going to blow a fuse! Remember the instruction to "love thy neighbor as thyself"? For me, it was easy to love my neighbor, I just forgot the "as thyself" part. Everyone is important . . . and that includes me as well!

I was able to step back and appreciate all the energy I was expending. I don't think that I had fully realized the enormous demands that all of the crystal and metaphysical and spiritual work was putting on my system. Now I could feel it just by noticing how weak I was. Lying in bed, I was able to take a closer look at all the dynamics that resulted in being where I was.

After this experience I realize very clearly something about helping: I couldn't help others unless I also helped myself. At the same time, I helped myself by helping others. It's a circle of giving and receiving. Anytime you're doing crystal ball gazing work or any other metaphysical or spiritual work, this circle of energy is vitally important. If you don't recharge, nurture, or otherwise take care of yourself, at some point you'll burn out.

Now, if you're only doing a reading every once in a while, you're not going to have much of a problem with burnout. Just be sure to give yourself time to rest after the reading. However, if you start doing a lot of readings for other people, or for yourself, you're going to need to put yourself on a regular recharging program. These days, unless there's a real emergency, I always take an hour or so every morning that is entirely *for me*. I do those things that are fun for me, usually reading books over a cup of tea, and just relaxing. I try to remember to drink lots of water and/or ginger tea because it will help keep my nervous system strong. If I'm sick or feeling weak for some reason, I don't do any crystal ball readings or crystal-healing work unless it's urgent. Practically speaking, I lightened up my schedule, making far fewer appointments during the day. I stopped traveling as much and hired people to assist me. I regularly use breathing practices and some of the others that are written in this book to help keep me calm and centered. (The long deep-breathing practice given in Chapter Four is excellent to use.) I also meditate, either silently or with meditation music. (I like to go "sound traveling.") I pay attention to myself, honoring my feelings and monitoring my energy system so that I stay in balance. If my nervous system is weak, for example, I'll do a practice for my navel center. If my heart feels closed, or my third eye, I'll do practices for those centers. Chapter Three talks about these energy centers and how you can use your crystal balls and color stones to open and balance them.

☺

THE NEXT STEP

I hope that these warnings don't scare you off. They're only meant as part of a framework that will help you crystal ball gaze successfully. Now all you have to do is use your crystal ball. You have all the information that you need to get going, and to have some pretty incredible experiences along the way. And it may possibly change your life. After all, a crystal ball is a seeing tool . . . it helps you see more, to extend your awareness. This is, after all, why it's been used for centuries. If you use your crystal ball with this information in hand, it may well change the way you perceive. As soon as you perceive more, your understanding changes, and so does your relationship with everything in your world. Ultimately, you change too . . . in ways from the spiritual to the practical.

Though there are certain generalities about crystal ball gazing, each person who uses a crystal ball has a unique experience every time. No two crystal ball readings are alike, just like no two moments in life are ever alike. They'll offer unique experiences tailored just for you.

Like any good tool, to get the most from it, it helps if you know what it's used for and how to use it. That's what this book is for. I hope this information is as inspiring as it is instructional. Having said this, what's the next step? Start using your crystal ball. Or if you've already started, keep using it . . . with a fresh mind and "new eyes" every time. Keep on gazing, even if you think you're not seeing anything, or imagining things, or even if you think that you've gone as far as you can or seen as much as you can. You haven't. For, like life, there's no end to it.

☙

A PARTING AFFIRMATION FOR EVERYDAY USE

Knowing that this is the last part of this book, I wanted to leave you with something that would be truly spectacular. The problem was that as soon as I started thinking that way, of course, I couldn't think of a thing to say! So I decided to gaze into the lighted crystal ball sitting next to me here on my table and do a minireading, asking the crystal ball for a good closing, something valuable that people can take with them after reading this book. Here is what happened:

What came through to me were first some visuals; one of a person pulling a crystal ball out of his pocket and looking into it, the other of a person looking into a large sphere and another of someone just feeling the sphere in her pocket. As I saw these visuals, I "heard" these words, which seemed to come right from the sphere into my heart. As I heard them, I felt a sense of assurance and peace sweep through me ... and the inner strength that comes from that. When I contemplated these words and the images that came to me, I realized that, unlike the inspiring story that I thought I would be writing, these words formed a powerful affirmation that would give you just the feeling I had when I first heard them; inner strength and a faith in oneself, peace, clarity, and energy.

The images also showed that instead of needing to set aside a special time to do this as a formal crystal ball meditation (which you could also do), you could at any time pick up your crystal ball, look into it or even just feel it, and say these words to yourself as a prayer and a reminder. You will see that this affirmation is formed into sections, actually several affirmations in one. Each section can stand alone, so if there's one that particularly resounds with you, or seems right for what you're experiencing in your life at the time, just use that. Use your crystal ball in this case, not just as a gazing tool, but also as a tool to refocus yourself in the whirlwind of life. Gaze into the crystal clear clarity of your sphere and let it be your reminder of the crystal clear clarity that is always there within the depths of your own being. Here is the affirmation.

Gazing into my crystal ball, I feel how ancient it is ... and still ... a quiet presence like the "Stone People" of the shaman. Looking into its depths, an interplay of cloud and light, solidity and space, I let my mind go free, tossing off all the fragments of half thought that were floating in my head. Now I ask this question: "What do the

Stone People have to say?" Quietly I wait, concentrating on the question, until I see images forming in the ball, in my mind's eye ... and I hear these words spill into my heart:

When you look into me,
Let me remind you of the infinite ways there are to see,
All of them true. Open your eyes.

When you see me, take a rest, a short break.
Let your mind go free for a few moments,
Abandoning all thinking.

As you look into me, breathe, and let go.
Don't think anything ... don't do anything ... don't be anything.
Now relax.

Look into me,
Go ahead and feel what you're feeling.
Rest your heart ... and say this to yourself,
   The love of the most heavenly being
   is with me at all times.
   I shall not fear.

For energy, gaze into me
And declare about yourself,
   I am the power of the wind,
   Yet clear and fresh as a gentle breeze.

If you're tired, sad, ill or afraid,
Open your eyes.
Look into me and repeat these words
That reflect the truth of your self:

   The creative fire of the universe is within me.
   The life-giving breath of the Higher Spirit shines
   Throughout me, within me and about me,
   A comfort and strength without end.

FURTHER RESOURCES

CRYSTAL BALLS AND LIGHTBOXES

The first thing that you'll want to do if you elect to further pursue crystal ball gazing is to purchase a crystal ball, if you don't have one already. There are many stores that carry crystal balls. Usually they are New Age or specialty gift stores. Sometimes you can even find them in rock shops. It is easier to read a crystal ball if it is lit, either by sunlight, candlelight, or by placing it on a lightbox. If you are having trouble finding a crystal ball and/or a lightbox in your area, feel free to call, fax, or write to my company and we can provide you with information about which stores are closest to you that carry them. Here is where you can find us:

UMA
2165 E. Francisco Blvd. Suite B
San Rafael, CA 94901
Phone: (415) 453-8845; Fax: (415) 453-1944

☺

The following is a list of books, music, and guided-visualization recordings that you can use either to help you in your crystal ball gazing or further increase what you've learned about various topics in this book. I have arranged them under various topics so you can more easily find what you're looking for.

BOOKS

ASTRAL BODIES AND ASTRAL TRAVEL

Astral Travel: Your Guide to the Secrets of Out-of-the-Body Experiences, Gaven and Yvonne Frost. York Beach, ME: Samuel Weiser Inc., 1986.
This is a good guidebook, with explanations of how to do it.

The Astral Body and Other Astral Phenomena, A. E. Powell. Wheaton, IL: The Theosophical Publishing House, 1927.
This is an excellent book explaining the astral world and astral travel in great detail. Also good by the same author are these books explaining the other nonphysical bodies and worlds: The Etheric Double, The Mental Body, *and* The Causal Body.

Subtle Body: Essence and Shadow, David Tansley. New York: Thames & Hudson, Inc., 1977.

COLOR

Color Therapy, Pauline Wills. Rockport, MA: Element, 1993.
This is a good explanation of the use of color for health and healing, its use with the chakra system, and exactly how it works to affect our bodies, minds, and emotions.

CRYSTALS AND STONES

Curious Lore of Precious Stones, G. F. Kunz. J. B. Lippincott, 1913. Reprinted by Dover Press, New York, 1970.

Clearing Crystal Consciousness, Christa Faye Burka. Albuquerque, NM: Brotherhood of Light, Inc., 1985.

Crystal Communion: Love Light Meditations, Sri Akhenaton. Columbia, MD: Portal Press, 1994.

Spiritual Value of Gemstones, Wallace G. Richardson as channeled through Lenora Huet. Devorss Pub. Co., 1980.

The Complete Crystal Guidebook, Uma Silbey. New York: Bantam, 1987.

The Crystal Book, Dael. Sunol, CA: The Crystal Co., 1983.

DREAMS

Dreams, Memories and Reflections, C. G. Jung. New York: Vintage Books, 1965.
This classic has lots of information about dreams, the collective unconscious, intuition, and psychology that should aid you in your understanding of these processes as well as help you with crystal ball interpretation.

Symbols of Transformation in Dreams, Jean Dalby Clift and Wallace B. Clift. New York: Crossroad, 1993.
This book talks about common dream symbols and motifs and their interpretations. It's oriented toward personal transformation using dreamwork. It's both practical and personal and will show you many parallels between crystal ball gazing work and dreamwork.

The Lucid Dreamer: A Waking Guide for the Traveler Between Worlds, Malcolm Godwin. New York: Simon & Schuster, 1994.
This is also a good guidebook, giving twenty exercises to enable you to experience conscious dreaming firsthand. It will also show you parallels between astral travel, dreamwork, and crystal ball gazing.

The Way of the Dream: On Jungian Dream Interpretation, Fraser Boa with Marie-Louise Von Franz. Boston, MA: Shambala Publications, 1988.
This is a collection of first person stories of dreams and their interpretations. It will help you with your crystal ball gazing interpretation.

EVERYDAY SPIRITUALITY AND PRACTICAL MYSTICISM

Enlightenment on the Run, Uma Silbey. San Rafael, CA: Airo Press, 1993.

A good overview of everyday, practical spirituality, discussing many of the issues that will come up for you in your gazing as well as in the rest of your life.

Mystics: The Soul's Journey into Truth, Andrew Harvey. San Francisco: HarperCollins, 1996.
This book will serve as a good introduction to many of the world's spiritual traditions and relates them all with each other. This well-written book is filled with examples of practical mysticism.

GENERAL INFORMATION: PSYCHICS, HISTORY, SCRYING (GAZING), ETC.

The following books will give you more information about some of the history of psychicism, crystal ball gazing and scrying, Gypsies, the occult, and the Inquisition. You will also find in these books true-life stories of modern-day gazers and psychics.

Divining the Future, Eva Shaw. New York: Facts On File, 1995.

Gypsies, Howard Greenfeld. New York: Crown Publishers, 1977.

Occult America, John Godwin. Garden City, NY:Doubleday & Company, 1972.

Psychics, editors of *Psychic Magazine.* New York: Harper & Row, 1972.

Telling Fortunes, Alvin Schwartz. New York: J. B. Lippincott, 1987.

The Fortune Tellers, Athene Williams et al. New York: Black Watch, 1974.

The Gypsies, Angus Fraser. Oxford, UK: Blackwell, 1992.

The Secrets of Foretelling Your Own Future, Maurice Woodruff. New York: The New American Library, Inc., in association with The World Publishing Company, 1969.

The Sybil Leek Book of Fortune Telling, Sybil Leek. Toronto, Ontario: The Macmillan Company, Collier/Macmillan Canada Ltd., 1969.

KUNDALINI ENERGY AND
SUBTLE ENERGY SYSTEMS

Kundalini Awakening: A Gentle Guide to Chakra Activation and Spiritual Growth, John Selby. New York: Bantam, 1992.
This is packed full of information that will help lead you to a greater understanding of the chakra systems; the power of mantras or "sacred sounds," breathing techniques for stress and relaxation, helpful meditations, and guided imagery.

The Serpent Power, Arthur Avalon. New York: Dover, 1974.
Though often a bit technical, this excellent book offers a complete explanation of subtle energy systems, mantras, and sound current meditation, etc.

MUSIC

Music and the Mind, Anthony Storr. New York: Ballantine Books, 1992.
This psychiatrist explains how music stimulates and affects the mind, captures the heart, and nurtures the soul.

SCIENCE AND SPIRITUALITY

These books speak from a scientific perspective to explain and support many of the metaphysical concepts and realities presented in this book.

Quantum Consciousness: The Guide to Experiencing Quantum Psychology, Stephen Wolinsky. Las Vegas: Bramble Books, 1993.
This fascinating book bridges quantum physics, meditation, and psychology, covering such topics as the nature of consciousness, time and space, nonordinary realities, matter and energy.

Parallel Universes: The Search For Other Worlds, Fred Alan Wolf. New York: Simon & Schuster, 1988.
This book forms a bridge between physics and mysticism, talking about

such topics as time travel, lucid dreaming, quantum physics, relativity, and black holes. It's very accessible, even for the unscientific.

The Spiritual Universe: How Quantum Physics Proves the Existence of the Soul, Fred Alan Wolf. New York: Simon & Schuster, 1996.

Taking the Quantum Leap, Fred Alan Wolf. New York: Harper & Row, 1989.
Again combining science and mysticism, this book deals with energy, consciousness, and quantum physics in such topics as the essential unity in life, being in two places at once, and the concept that "we are the whole universe." Again, it's quite accessible.

SYMBOLISM

These books should serve to open your mind so that you are more easily able to "see" symbolically, a talent so crucial to crystal ball gazing. They will also suggest lots of symbols to you that you can look for in your reading.

Symbolism Through the Ages, Kathryn Davis Henry. Los Angeles: The Theosophical Research Society, 1988.
Examines both legends and artifacts to show other ways of looking at animals, the elements, and nature. This offers a good synopsis of some common symbols.

The Secret Language of Symbols: A Visual Key to Symbols and Their Meanings, David Fontana. San Francisco: Chronicle Books, 1994.
An interesting and well-written book with 300 full-color illustrations combining art and essays that explore the web of culture, history, and psychology and their place in our psyche.

RECORDINGS

All of these music and guided-visualization recordings are excellent to use in conjunction with your crystal ball gazing and will in some way help you to be more effective in your reading. Once you are focused into your crystal ball, listen to the guided visualization and its effect will be tremendously amplified. The music is designed to help bring you into the trance state, or once you are thus focused, to deepen and extend your trance state. Some of this music is what I call "journey music." With this type of music, gaze into your crystal ball while you listen to it and let the sound lead you to an inner soundscape of visual imagery, unblocked emotions, heightened awareness and insight. Other recordings are designed to open your heart and calm your mind, bringing you to a state of deep inner peace that will help you in your gazing. Most of this music you can find (or request) in New Age or specialty gift stores or in some of the larger music stores. If you are unable to find these selections, I have included information about where you can purchase them directly. Enjoy!

MUSIC: INSTRUMENTAL

Aeterna, Constance Demby. Hearts of Space, P.O. Box 31321, San Francisco, CA 94131; (fax) 415-759-1166 or Sound Currents, P.O. Box 1044, Fairfax, CA 94978.
This gives you the feeling of being in a cathedral, listening to the magnificent music of the angels. All synthesized. Uplifting.

Chambers of the Heart, Aeoliah. Helios Music, P.O. Box 374, Mt. Shasta, CA 96067.
Piano and keyboard music that's filled with love and passion.

Concept for a Dream, Jay Scott Berry. CSI, P.O. Box 126, Buckingham, VA 23921.
A lighthearted recording suggesting a magical fairyland of dreams. Uplifting. Also recommended is his recording Symphony of Light.

Eight String Religion, David Darling. Hearts of Space, P.O. Box 31321, San Francisco, CA 94131; (fax) 415-1166.
A very beautiful recording with acoustic cello, piano, voice, and some envi-

ronmental sounds. *Warm, beautiful, and emotional. Great for reaching deep into the emotions.*

Honorable Sky, Peter Kater & R. Carlos Nakai. Silver Wave Records, P.O. Box 7943, Boulder, CO 80306; (303) 443-5617.
An intimate improvisational interweaving of piano, Native American flute, cellos, oboe, eagle bone, pennywhistle, and soprano sax. Enlivening, heartful, and beautiful.

Inner Peace, Steven Halpern. Inner Peace Music, P.O. Box 2644, San Anselmo, CA 94979-2644.
Soothing and uplifting keyboard music ranging from solo to orchestral. Also nice by him are Crystal Suite *and* Gifts of the Angels.

Music for Relaxation, Jim Oliver. The Relaxation Company, 20 Lumber Road, Roslyn, NY 11576.
Sounds that soothe, for relaxation of body and mind.

Novus Magnificat, Constance Demby. Sound Currents, P.O. Box 1044, Fairfax, CA 94978.
Contemporary classical sacred symphonic space music, called the "Mozart Requiem of the New Age." A transformative cosmic journey that will uplift your spirit.

Preludes: Music of Serenity, assorted artists. World Disc Music Sampler, P.O. Box 2749, Friday Harbor, WA 98250; (800) 228-5711.
Features some of the lighter, quieter compositions by some of the World Disc musicians. Guitars, flutes, keyboards prevail to peaceful effect.

Slow Diver, Tom Vedvik. Higher Octave; (800) 562-8283.
A very soothing and gentle ambient soundscape. All synthesized.

Till the End of Time, Stephan Micus. JAPO/ECM Records, Gleichmannstr. 10, Munchen 60, Germany.
A hauntingly beautiful recording with table harp, zither, and acoustic guitar. Also good is his recording Koan.

Watergarden, Uma. Blue Sky/Airo Audio, 2165 E. Francisco Blvd., Suite B, San Rafael, CA 94901; (800) 654-9357.

An enchanting, angelically heartful, and peaceful recording with strings, bells, and chimes. Heartful, healing, and beautiful.

JOURNEY MUSIC

This music ranges from the soft sounds of actual nature recordings, "otherworldly" synthesizer, to trance drumming. Some is purely instrumental and some is vocal. Enter your crystal ball, let your mind go, and let the music carry you.

Dawn and Dusk by a Mountain Stream, Richard Hooper. World Disc Recordings, 915 Spring St., Friday Harbor, WA 98250; (800) 228-5711. *This is a recording of nature sounds that are very soothing. Ask for their catalogue of other nature recordings.*

Edges of the Soul, Harold Moses. Crucible Sound, P.O. Box 19191, Boulder, CO 80508; (303) 784-5941. *The music of viola and synthesizer recorded live. A journey into the heart.*

Jiva Mukti, Nada Shakti and Bruce BecVar. Shining Star Prod.; (800) 987-9988. *Vocal and instrumental journey music using a blend of percussion, keyboards, and harp. Uses Tibetan and Sanskrit mantras and unique composition for a lush soundscape.*

Medicine Songs, the Creek Medicine Man Bearheart. Airo Audio, 2165 E. Francisco Blvd., Suite B, San Rafael, CA 94901; (800) 654-9357. *Songs of the Native American Peyote lodge (Native American Church), combined with sounds of the elements and spirit animals, drum, rattle, and Native American flute to take you traveling beyond the physical world into the realms of the nonordinary.*

Sacred Spirit Drums and *Sacred Earth Drums,* David and Steve Gordon. Sequoia Records, P.O. Box 280, Topanga, CA 90290; (800) 524-5513. *Shamanic drumming combined with Native American flute, the sounds of nature, and Incan pan pipes take you on a shamanic journey to the inner realms.*

Soma, Steve Roach and Robert Rich. Hearts of Space, P.O. Box 31321, San Francisco, CA 94131.
An otherworldly yet ancient sound combining synthesizers, flutes, ocarinas, acoustic guitar, and various percussion. Very mystical trance journeying music.

Voyager, Uma. Airo Audio, 2165 E. Francisco Blvd., Suite B, San Rafael, CA 94901; (800) 654-9357.
Layered female vocals and instrumental compositions combine to take you traveling through the angelic planes, into deep space, and deep into your heart. Songs of love to the Higher Spirit are those that evolve naturally and spontaneously from an open heart. Magical and deeply emotional. Combining the sounds and rhythms of the East and West.

VOCAL
(INCLUDES INSTRUMENTATION)

Gloria, Robert Gass and On Wings of Song. Spring Hill Music, P.O. Box 800, Boulder, CO 80306.
Choral music with an angelic feeling. Uplifting and peaceful. Heartful.

Heart of Perfect Wisdom, Robert Gass and On Wings of Song. Spring Hill Music, P.O. Box 800, Boulder, CO 80306.
Chants from the Buddhist "Heart Sutra" blend with Tibetan overtone chanting, bells and Nepalese bamboo flutes for a lush and heartful sound tapestry designed for inner peace.

Om Namah Sivaya, Robert Gass and On Wings of Song. Spring Hill Music, P.O. Box 800, Boulder, CO 80306.
Designed for spiritual uplift, it's very peaceful. Female choral music. Ask for their catalogue because most of their other recordings would be good to use.

Heart of Peace, Uma. Airo Audio, 2165 E. Francisco Blvd., Suite B, San Rafael, CA 94901; (800) 654-9357.
Combination of synthesized tones, tamboura, sensitive percussion, and

ancient Sanskrit chants for a mystical, heartful feeling. Designed to carry you beyond the physical. Let the sound carry you and let go.

Spiritus, Lorellei. Soundings of the Planet, P.O. Box 43512, Tucson, AZ 85733; (520) 792-9888.
Female angelic-sounding vocals along with keyboards, flutes, violin, and light percussion. Lush orchestration with multilayered sound. Inspiring.

GUIDED VISUALIZATIONS

The Cauldron Journey for Healing, Nicki Scully with music by Roland Barker and Jerry Garcia. P.O. Box 5025, Eugene, OR 97405; (503) 484-1099.
Side one takes you to your spirit guide then to the island of Kuan Yin to receive healing. Based on the ancient Egyptian mystery schools. Designed for healing work with AIDS and leukemia, it is also effective for any range of healing needed. Side two is music only.

Crystal Path, Uma with Ramana Das. Airo Audio, 2165 E. Francisco Blvd., Suite B, San Rafael, CA 94901; (800) 654-9357.
Meant to be used with crystal and crystal ball gazing. Side one guides you into the crystal (or crystal ball), to experience heightened states of energy, open your heart, communicate on the inner planes, and reach deep levels of calm. Side two empowers you to even deeper levels of heightened awareness and attunement for healing work with yourself or others.

Crystals, Chakras, Colors and Sound, Uma with Ramana Das. Airo Audio, 2165 E. Francisco Blvd., Suite B, San Rafael, CA 94901; (800) 654-9357.
Two guided visualizations to focus the amplifying energy of crystals and crystal balls with color, imagery, and sound toning to activate the seven main chakras and sensitize, balance, and utilize your subtle energy channels. Instructional as well as deeply experiential.

Healing, Uma. Airo Audio, 2165 E. Francisco Blvd., Suite B, San Rafael, CA 94901; (800) 654-9357.
Designed for healing the physical body as well as to discover and change the

emotional and mental underpinnings that support illness or dis-ease. Experience shimmering waves of sound, an astral healing chamber, angelic beings, light and sound. Energizing and deeply peaceful.

Journey to the Golden Pyramid, Richard Gordon with Gail G. Barber on harp. Creative Productions Inc., 4155 Essen Lane, #234, Baton Rouge, LA 70809; (504) 927-8899; or reach Gail at P.O. Box 53190, Lubbock, TX 79453; (806) 799-3320.
A guided meditation with voice and harp that "allows you to journey to the farthest reaches of your heart and mind."

LOVE, available from Airo Audio in both CD and cassette. 2165 E. Francisco Blvd., Suite B, San Rafael, CA 94901; (800) 654-9357.
Guided imagery with heartfelt background music to open your heart to love . . . for yourself and others. Powerful forgiveness and loving-kindness meditations gently lift self-imposed blockages to the experience of love. Ancient breath and color meditations deepen the bonding with another.

Opening the Heart, Robert Gass and On Wings of Song. Spring Hill Music, P.O. Box 800, Boulder, CO 80306.
Side one is guided meditation with music, with such visualizations as "The Rose," "Perhaps Love," and "Welcome to This World." Side two is music alone. Peaceful and heart-opening, just as the title suggests.

The Power to Heal Is Within You, Susan Justice. P.O. Box 765, Woodacre, CA 94973; (415) 258-0509.
A heartfelt healing journey by a woman who faced serious illness herself and used this meditation (as well as other techniques) to heal herself. Music as well as voice. Leaves you with a sense of deep peace and balance.

PROSPERITY, available from Airo Audio in both CD and cassette. 2165 E. Francisco Blvd., Suite B, San Rafael, CA 94901; (800) 654-9357
Imagery and affirmations combine with sound to connect you energetically with the endless stream of abundance and universal life force to bring you prosperity. Included are meditations to help you identify and release the barriers that keep you from being prosperous and bring the energy and vision to manifest your dreams.

Relax, Uma. Airo Audio, 2165 E. Francisco Blvd., Suite B, San Rafael, CA 94901; (800) 654-9357.
Go into your crystal ball and let the voice and music guide you. Side one relaxes your physical body while side two calms your emotions and thoughts. Good for developing focus as well as destressing from a busy life. Heartful and effective.

Vision Quest, Creek Medicine Man Bearheart. Airo Audio, 2165 E. Francisco Blvd., Suite B, San Rafael, CA 94901; (800) 654-9357.
Side one leads listeners in an inner vision quest to each of the seven sacred directions for their energy and vision. Meet spirit guides, and receive answers to that which you seek. Side two creates an actual ceremony with the prayers and songs that are actually done in a traditional vision quest. Very beautiful as well as empowering.

Known for introducing crystals in the early eighties and as the author of the bestseller *The Complete Crystal Guidebook,* Uma draws from over thirty years of focused spiritual practice and metaphysical training as well as her everyday life experiences of being a mother and wife, a business owner, recording artist, and writer. Raised as a Christian, she has since studied, meditated, and taken initiation with Hindu, Sikh, and Buddhist masters as well as with Native American shamans and medicine men. Besides being a nationally acknowledged "stone healer," she is a practitioner of Vipassana and sound current meditation, pranayam, and devotional singing (kirtan). A teacher of kundalini yoga, Uma also received initiation into the Buddhist Kalachakra and Mahamudra practices. She has completed four vision quests, is a pipe holder, is authorized to "pour water" (or be in charge of) the Native American inippi or sweat-lodge ceremony, and has been trained in Native American and other indigenous healing ways.

Believing that the way to wisdom is not to remain secluded but to balance spirituality with everyday living, Uma has done just that. She holds a degree from the University of California at Los Angeles and is a successful writer, happily married, with two children. Since 1980, she has headed the phenomenally successful UMA Jewelry Co. which specializes in her crystal and natural gemstone "transformational jewelry" and handheld stone "power totems." She has recorded and composed ten albums of meditation music, "journey" music, and guided visualizations for her own music label, Airo Audio. Over the years, her articles and interviews have appeared in dozens of publications worldwide, her appearances have been broadcast nationally on both TV and radio, and her compositions have been played on both national and overseas radio.

Having "a foot in both worlds," Uma is uniquely qualified as a teacher and spokesperson who synthesizes mysticism and spirituality with the rational pragmatism and demands of modern living.